W9-CBU-232

DISEASES & DISORDERS

Tourette Syndrome

Titles in the Diseases & Disorders series include:

DISEASES & DISORDERS

Tourette Syndrome

Sheila Wyborny

LUCENT BOOKS
A part of Gale, Cengage Learning

GALE
CENGAGE Learning

Detroit • New York • San Francisco • New Haven, Conn • Waterville, Maine • London

LIBRARY OF CONGRESS CATALOGING-IN-PUBLICATION DATA

Wyborny, Sheila, 1950-
 Tourette syndrome / by Sheila Wyborny.
  p. cm. -- (Diseases & disorders)
 Includes bibliographical references and index.
 ISBN 978-1-4205-0280-0 (hardcover)
 1. Tourette syndrome--Juvenile literature. I. Title.
 RC375.W93 2010
 616.8'3--dc22
                                                          2010018792

Lucent Books
27500 Drake Rd.
Farmington Hills, MI 48331

ISBN-13: 978-1-4205-0280-0
ISBN-10: 1-4205-0280-8

Printed in the United States of America
2 3 4 5 6 7 14 13 12 11 10

Printed by Bang Printing, Brainerd, MN, 2nd Ptg., 11/2010

Table of Contents

"The Most Difficult Puzzles Ever Devised"

Charles Best, one of the pioneers in the search for a cure for diabetes, once explained what it is about medical research that intrigued him so. "It's not just the gratification of knowing one is helping people," he confided, "although that probably is a more heroic and selfless motivation. Those feelings may enter in, but truly, what I find best is the feeling of going toe to toe with nature, of trying to solve the most difficult puzzles ever devised. The answers are there somewhere, those keys that will solve the puzzle and make the patient well. But how will those keys be found?"

Since the dawn of civilization, nothing has so puzzled people—and often frightened them, as well—as the onset of illness in a body or mind that had seemed healthy before. A seizure, the inability of a heart to pump, the sudden deterioration of muscle tone in a small child—being unable to reverse such conditions or even to understand why they occur was unspeakably frustrating to healers. Even before there were names for such conditions, even before they were understood at all, each was a reminder of how complex the human body was, and how vulnerable.

While our grappling with understanding diseases has been frustrating at times, it has also provided some of humankind's most heroic accomplishments. Alexander Fleming's accidental discovery in 1928 of a mold that could be turned into penicillin has resulted in the saving of untold millions of lives. The isolation of the enzyme insulin has reversed what was once a death sentence for anyone with diabetes. There have been great strides in combating conditions for which there is not yet a cure, too. Medicines can help AIDS patients live longer, diagnostic tools such as mammography and ultrasounds can help doctors find tumors while they are treatable, and laser surgery techniques have made the most intricate, minute operations routine.

This "toe-to-toe" competition with diseases and disorders is even more remarkable when seen in a historical continuum. An astonishing amount of progress has been made in a very short time. Just two hundred years ago, the existence of germs as a cause of some diseases was unknown. In fact, it was less than 150 years ago that a British surgeon named Joseph Lister had difficulty persuading his fellow doctors that washing their hands before delivering a baby might increase the chances of a healthy delivery (especially if they had just attended to a diseased patient)!

Each book in Lucent's Diseases and Disorders series explores a disease or disorder and the knowledge that has been accumulated (or discarded) by doctors through the years. Each book also examines the tools used for pinpointing a diagnosis, as well as the various means that are used to treat or cure a disease. Finally, new ideas are presented—techniques or medicines that may be on the horizon.

Frustration and disappointment are still part of medicine, for not every disease or condition can be cured or prevented. But the limitations of knowledge are being pushed outward constantly; the "most difficult puzzles ever devised" are finding challengers every day.

When Misbehavior Is Actually a Disorder

Many people have never even heard of Tourette syndrome (TS). Those who have generally have a mental image of a person thrashing about, grimacing, and cursing. Because of this prevailing idea, TS is sometimes called the cursing disease. When characters in movies and on television are portrayed with TS, they are usually shown making bizarre facial gestures, jerking and flailing their arms and legs, and cursing loudly. Although it is true that some people with TS experience bouts of cursing, this particular symptom is actually quite rare among people with the disorder. Some people have mild symptoms, such as blinking, twitching, or grunting softly. In fact, some people have symptoms so mild that their daily lives are not impaired at all. The more bizarre symptoms, however, are the ones that attract attention, sometimes very negative attention.

Misunderstood

People suffering from Tourette syndrome can be seriously misunderstood by those who do not know them and do not know they have this condition. Strangers may stare, point, or even laugh when a person experiences a bout of symptoms. This misunderstanding is caused by the public's general lack of knowledge. The sudden bouts of physical or vocal behaviors that are often mistaken for inappropriate behavior are actually symptoms of TS, which is a type of neurological disorder. A neurological disorder is a disease of the central nervous system. In the case of TS, the brain is the part of the central nervous system that is affected.

The impact of TS on those who suffer from it is twofold. First, the person must deal with the disorder and its symptoms. Secondly, the person has to deal with the reactions of others if the symptoms occur in a public place. This causes some people who suffer from TS to become withdrawn. One sympathetic doctor describes it this way: "One of the worst aspects of this condition is the lack of public awareness of it and the unjustified hurtful blaming of innocent patients for behavior not of their making."[1]

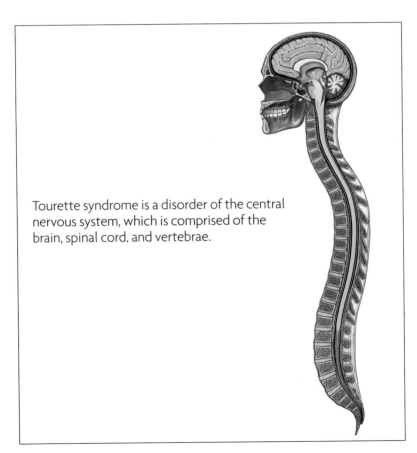

Tourette syndrome is a disorder of the central nervous system, which is comprised of the brain, spinal cord, and vertebrae.

When a Behavior Becomes a Disorder

Some people, both children and adults, choose to act out and misbehave. For instance, an adult might become angry with someone and drive recklessly. A child may behave in a disruptive manner in the classroom by making noises, shouting, banging on a desk, or even cursing. In most cases of this behavior, the person chooses to behave inappropriately. Yet people with TS usually have little or no control over these actions. These movements, behaviors, and vocalizations are involuntary. This means that these people are not doing these things on purpose, and it is extremely difficult, sometimes impossible, to control the symptoms.

These behaviors may range from bouts of rapid eye blinking and throat clearing to grimacing, cursing, or repeating other socially unacceptable phrases. For those suffering from TS, these bouts are usually preceded by feelings similar to the need to scratch or to sneeze. Some people describe it as a building of physical tension, a tightness between the shoulders, or energy that finally becomes so strong that it has to be released in some way, like steam building in a tea kettle until the kettle begins to whistle.

Better Times for Tourette Syndrome Patients

There is no really good time to have TS or any other potentially serious disorder. Today, however, knowledge about the condition and treatment options—ranging from drugs that lessen the severity and frequency of the bouts to psychotherapies that help patients cope with them—allow those with TS to lead much more normal, stable lives than patients of earlier centuries. For instance, just a couple of centuries ago people exhibiting the symptoms later known as TS might have been flogged, thrown into prison, or even burned at the stake for being witches or possessed by demons. The people of those days tended to treat anything they did not understand as something evil, something that needed to be driven out or destroyed. They did not know that the outbursts were symptoms of a medical problem, so they tried to get rid of them by killing or maiming the person with the disorder.

Later, poor people showing signs of what is now known as TS were locked up in insane asylums. The very wealthy dealt with this condition by keeping the family member in an isolated part of the family home or sending them to live someplace in the country, away from other people.

Although the symptoms of TS have affected people for centuries, the condition was not identified as a medical disorder or given a name until the late 1800s. The disorder was named in honor of Georges Gilles de la Tourette, the physician who identified it. In 1884 de la Tourette wrote an article about the mysterious condition in which he described the compulsive tics, spasmodic twitching of facial muscles, and vocalizations of several different patients. He described these people as mostly intelligent, except for the bouts of tics that were usually brief and did not impede their ability to feed themselves or otherwise attend to their own personal needs.

Although there is still a certain amount of social stigma associated with TS, research and programs to educate people about the disorder are making the world a more tolerant and accepting place for people with this misunderstood condition.

CHAPTER ONE

What Is Tourette Syndrome?

Knowing the facts about Tourette syndrome (TS) is important both for the person with the condition and for friends and family who love and care about him or her. Understanding the condition and its symptoms can make the situation less frightening for the TS patient when bouts of tics occur. Understanding the symptoms of the condition can also help family and friends to be more patient with those affected by TS, particularly if they know that the tics are involuntary.

What It Is and Who Is Affected

TS is a neurological disorder. A neurological disorder means that some part of the brain is affected. It is a noncontagious, nonfatal condition that, at this time, can be treated but cannot be cured. It does not affect a person's life span or intelligence, and most people who have TS go to school, hold jobs, and lead full lives. TS can be found among all races and ethnic groups. Some studies indicate that up to two hundred thousand people in the United States have moderate to severe symptoms, and it is believed that an additional 1 million experience mild symptoms. Sometimes the condition is so mild that it is never actually diagnosed. Among school-age children in the United States, it is estimated that about 1 percent of mainstream students between the ages of five and sixteen have mild to severe TS. Worldwide it is estimated that up to 85 billion people have TS to some degree.

The many different kinds of noises, words, grimaces, and physical movements associated with TS are called tics. Tics are the outward symptoms of TS. Tics can occur in any part of the body at any time. They are involuntary, hard-to-control muscle movements that come on unexpectedly, with little or no warning. Tics are caused by the spasmodic movement of muscles that control arm and leg movement, facial expression,

Tourette syndrome affects the brain in ways that cause involuntary physical reactions, such as tics and spasms, as well as verbal noises like grunts.

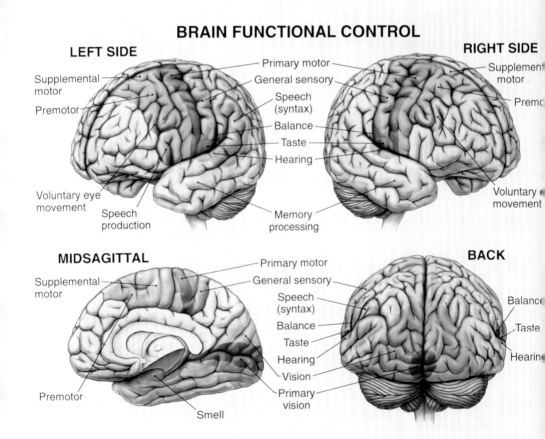

BRAIN FUNCTIONAL CONTROL

LEFT SIDE

- Supplemental motor
- Premotor
- Voluntary eye movement
- Speech production

RIGHT SIDE

- Supplemental motor
- Premotor
- Voluntary eye movement

- Primary motor
- General sensory
- Speech (syntax)
- Balance
- Taste
- Hearing
- Memory processing

MIDSAGITTAL

- Supplemental motor
- Premotor
- Smell

BACK

- Balance
- Taste
- Hearing

- Primary motor
- General sensory
- Speech (syntax)
- Balance
- Taste
- Hearing
- Vision
- Primary vision

In Good Company

As Georges Gilles de la Tourette once said, most people who have Tourette syndrome are quite intelligent. In fact, a number of famous people from history have suffered from TS. For example, eighteenth-century essayist Samuel Johnson, a prolific writer and poet of his day, had TS. Additionally, some experts believe the composer Wolfgang Amadeus Mozart also suffered from TS.

More recently, former *Saturday Night Live* member Dan Ackroyd, the star of the films *Ghostbusters* and *The Blues Brothers*, went public with his childhood struggles with TS and Asperger's syndrome. Additionally, retired Major League Baseball player Jim Eisenreich, who played with the 1997 World Series champions, the Florida Marlins, suffered from TS. Eisenreich went through his entire childhood undiagnosed. His condition was not identified until he was twenty-three years old. Before his diagnosis, his symptoms had become so severe that he almost lost his career. Now retired from baseball, Eisenreich volunteers much of his time to educate the public about his neurological disorder.

Mahmoud Abdul-Raul (formerly Chris Jackson) is another successful sports figure who has TS. Abdul-Raul is a leading free-throw shooter in the National Basketball Association. He appeared in a documentary about TS called *Twitch and Shout*.

Wolfgang Amadeus Mozart, a renowned composer, is believed to have had Tourette's.

and even the voice. These motor, or movement, and vocal tics can range from simple to complex.

These symptoms usually appear in children between the ages of six and nine, although some symptoms occasionally appear earlier. Symptoms can range from twitchy body movements and facial tics, such as squinting and eye blinking, to vocal tics, such as throat clearing, grunting, and, in some cases, growling, howling, or swearing. For most people, the symptoms begin to diminish between the ages of sixteen and eighteen, although some people experience symptoms into adulthood. One TS patient, now an adult, describes when and how his symptoms began:

> My first symptoms appeared at age six. I bit my lip. My parents thought I had a speech problem, so I was off to a speech pathologist. Other than not pronouncing my S's and P's, she couldn't find anything wrong. Thinking the biting was a mental health issue, she suggested sending me to a psychologist. Then barking and other noises and movements started. Five years later I got diagnosed only because my parents read about someone in the paper and tracked down the doctor who had diagnosed the person.[2]

This young man's parents spent many frustrating years trying to find answers for their son's condition, and their child spent years being misunderstood. Although medical professionals do not have all of the answers about this disorder, at least progress has been made in diagnosis and treatment thanks to the research efforts of many scientists and physicians. Even if some answers are not 100 percent certain, they do at least provide clues about this disorder.

One thing scientists have learned is that other disorders can occur in conjunction with Tourette syndrome. One of the disorders most frequently associated with TS is attention deficit/hyperactivity disorder (ADHD). The attention deficit part of ADHD causes people to be easily distracted and have difficulty focusing on tasks. Hyperactivity is acting out on impulse rather than on thought and reason. For instance, a student with ADHD may grab a handful of papers off the teacher's desk and throw them into the air or suddenly run and tackle another student in the hallway. Without proper diagnosis, such actions can be mistaken for deliberately disruptive behavior.

Troublesome Tics

Tics usually occur in bursts or bouts. This means that the person will make not one but several motions or sounds during these bouts. Tics can be vocal, involving the voice, or motor, involving physical movement. Simple motor tics include facial grimaces, shoulder shrugs, neck jerks, and eye blinks. Complex motor tics are more pronounced and troublesome. Although these tics may appear purposeful, they are, in fact, involuntary. These are the types of tics that tend to draw a lot of attention. This attention can cause problems and embarrassment for the person with TS. Some of the complex motor tics, like hitting and biting, are violent and may cause harm to other people in the vicinity. Other complex motor tics include jumping and making obscene gestures, called copropraxia, and self-injury, such as picking at skin until it bleeds or biting and hitting oneself.

Some complex motor tics can be particularly embarrassing. These tics cause the person to compulsively grab, touch, lick, kiss, or hug other people, sometimes complete strangers. These are called extracorporeal phantom tics. The person with TS has impulses that lead him or her to believe that other people or objects are given some sort of relief by one of these types of physical contact. This can be threatening to a stranger, particularly if the person doing the grabbing is an older teenager or an adult.

Other examples of vocal tics often confused with inappropriate behavior include spitting, whistling, belching, humming, grunting, and wordless yelling. Among the complex vocal tics are "broken record" tics such as echolalia, which means repeating the last phrase, sound, or word spoken by another person, and palilalia, which is repeating one's own words or phrases. Other vocal tics, called nonobscene socially inappropriate behavior, involve words or phrases that are socially inappropriate, such as remarks about someone's physical appearance, race, or ethnicity. Still other complex vocal tics include making animal sounds, such as barking; repeating words or phrases out of context, such as commercial jingles from television and radio; and coprolalia, which involves shouting out obscene words or phrases. Although coprolalia is the tic most often portrayed in movies or television dramas about people with TS, it is actually one of the rarest tics. In fact, bouts of cursing or saying other inappropriate words or phrases, such as ethnic or racial slurs, occur in less than 15 percent of the people who have the disorder.

A doctor with Tourette syndrome, right, repeatedly touches the heads and shoulders of his sons. The display of tics is captured by small lights affixed to his fingers.

Tourette Syndrome in Movies and Media

In 2008 a Hallmark Hall of Fame movie titled *Front of the Class* was based on teacher/author Brad Cohen's book *Front of the Class: How Tourette Syndrome Made Me the Teacher I Never Had.* Besides writing and teaching, Cohen takes an active role in camp programs for young TS patients.

In the movie, *Everyone Loves Raymond* costar Patricia Heaton plays the mother of Cohen. Her character is initially blamed for her son's condition, with her divorce as a contributing factor. Heaton later spoke highly of Brad Cohen and stated that the movie was not just a movie about TS; it was also about the victory of the human spirit.

In addition to a made-for-TV movie, other broadcasts in recent years have also been devoted to bringing TS out into the open. One of these was a 2007 ABC *20/20* report titled "Growing Up with Tourette's." This report is part of a segment about children growing up with special challenges. Another production was the HBO documentary *I Have Tourette's but Tourette's Doesn't Have Me.* This HBO family feature examines the lives of several American children growing up with TS.

In addition to vocal and motor tics, some people with TS report experiencing nonobservable tics called internal tics. These tics are said to involve internal organs. Yet because these tics cannot be observed, there has been no research to study them; thus, other than the fact they have been reported by some people with TS, nothing else is currently known about them.

Both vocal and motor tics can change in the same person over time. In fact, some people experience bouts of tics that last only a few weeks or months and then go away entirely. Tics can also wax and wane. This means they can get better and worse over a period of time. The waxing and waning of tics occurs as a person's body grows and changes over time. The tics themselves can change. One tic may go away, but a new and totally different tic may take its place. These changes occur without warning, and the person has no control over them.

The Degrees of Impact

The extent to which TS affects a person's life depends on the severity and frequency of his or her tics. Because of this, TS sufferers are caught in a vicious cycle: The fear of having a bout of tics in public can cause stress and thereby bring on more tics. One adult, teacher Brad Cohen, who experiences disruptive tics, describes his fear of causing a scene at the funeral of a beloved student: "I wasn't sure if I wanted to go to the funeral because, as a person with Tourette's, I had not attended many funerals. My barking was sure to be prominent at a stressful time like this, and added to all the grief over the death of a child, it might make my presence too much for everyone."[3]

Any number of these tics could be mistaken for "crazy" or inappropriate behavior and cause problems for a child or an adult. Although someone with TS can learn to delay these outbursts to some degree, trying to hold them in can be very difficult. One TS patient describes the difficulty of holding back a tic and finally the sense of release after "letting go": "It's a feeling of having an itch on one's back you can't reach, the tension building. Then there's the symptom and the feeling of, 'Whew, it's out.'"[4]

The frequency and severity of tics can also be affected by changes in diet, routine, and environment. For instance, a move to a new town and a new job or school would certainly impact a person's routine and environment. Such an event can escalate tic activity, which can have a negative impact on students, who do not want to appear different in any way, and on workers, who want to make a good first impression in their new jobs. Additionally, extreme emotions such as anger, stress, excitement, fear, grief, and depression can bring on tics.

A number of foods, additives, and environmental factors can also cause tics. Dairy products, wheat, sweets, artificial colors

Dairy products such as milk, cheese, and yogurt may contribute to tics in Tourette's sufferers.

and flavors, and preservatives used in some food products trigger tics in some people. Caffeine, as is found in coffee, chocolate, and some soft drinks, can bring them on as well. Additionally, mold, scented products, fabric softeners, smoke, fumes from fuels, products used in home renovations, and pollens can trigger tics. Because so many different foods and environmental substances can trigger tics, many physicians suggest that people with TS keep track of what they were eating or drinking as well as what environmental factors may have been present when a bout of tics began. This log can help the physician and patient determine possible triggers and ways to avoid them.

In most cases, people with Tourette syndrome who develop tics begin experiencing mild motor or vocal tics as early as age three but usually between ages six and ten. The milder tics, such as throat clearing and eye blinking, are the most common beginning tics, although any kind can develop as the disorder progresses. As hormones change in early adolescence, the tics may worsen. Adolescents are already very concerned about their bodies, and they do not want to be "different," so the constant worry over having a bout of tics in public can increase their emotional stress considerably. On a positive note, however, young teens with TS tend to become more aware of what is going on with their bodies, and some are able to sense the premonitory urge, the beginning tension and anxiety experienced when a tic is building.

There are many kinds of these warning signals. They include, but are not limited to, a burning in the eyes before an eye blink tic, the feeling of a crick in the neck before a neck jerk or neck roll tic, dryness in the throat before coughing or throat clearing tics, and a tight feeling in arm and leg muscles before arm or leg extension tics.

Tics are more likely to occur when a person is tired or stressed and less likely to happen when he or she is relaxed, sleeping, or engaged in an interesting or enjoyable activity. With this new awareness, a person can learn to identify some of the feelings and situations that can bring on tics. He or she can then either avoid the tics or perhaps hold them back until a private spot, such as a restroom, quiet hallway, or vacant office, can be found in which to release them.

Friends, family, teachers, and classmates of people who have Tourette syndrome need to bear in mind that tics are not behavior. Instead, they are outward symptoms of the condition. The tics, such as obscenities or racial slurs, have absolutely nothing to do with how that person actually feels about other people. These tics are out of the person's control, just as the involuntary, jerky movements people with Parkinson's disease or cerebral palsy experience. If the person with TS knows that friends, family, and classmates are supportive and not judgmental about the tics, his or her stress will be lessened, and any decrease in emotional stress can help reduce the frequency and severity of the tics.

Tourette Syndrome: A Puzzle

Tourette syndrome is a neurological disorder—a condition that affects the brain and other parts of the central nervous system. It can be passed along through families, although all members of a family with a history of the condition do not necessarily inherit it. In recent years scientists have actually isolated a gene found in the central nervous system that they believe is connected to TS. A gene is a bit of DNA that determines traits. This particular gene has been labeled SLITRK1. This gene is involved in the growth of nerve cells. Located in the basal ganglia, cortex, and frontal lobes of the brain, some scientists believe that SLITRK1 may be a major TS connection.

Despite the fact that TS is inherited, there is good news for the children of parents who have TS. Just because a parent may have this gene and have symptoms of TS, there is only a 50 percent chance that the child of this parent will inherit the gene. This means that the child is just as likely to not inherit the condition as he or she is to inherit it. Additionally, inheriting the gene does not necessarily mean that the child will ever develop symptoms severe enough to need medical intervention. Severe symptoms appear in a small minority, only about 10 percent of those who inherit the gene. This means that the odds are much greater that children of a parent with Tourette syndrome will never require treatment for the disorder.

Tourette syndrome was once thought to be an "orphan disease," or a very rare disorder, but according to some recent statistics, approximately one in twenty-five hundred people in the United States has some degree of TS. Additionally, according to some studies, boys are about two to four times more likely than girls to develop this condition. Some researchers believe the male hormone, testosterone, may be a contributing

A woman prepares DNA samples for testing. Genetic research into Tourette syndrome identified the gene SLITRK1 as having a possible connection to the disease.

factor. Other studies indicate that anywhere between 30 and 60 percent of people who have TS also have some other type of disorder, such as obsessive-compulsive disorder or a learning disability such as ADHD.

Although most people who have TS inherit it, this is not the only way people develop this disorder. In some cases of Tourette syndrome, no known family origin has been identified. This type of TS occurs sporadically.

Research indicates that an infection in the body may cause some people to develop the sporadic form of TS. A streptococcal infection (strep) is one type of infection that has been studied in connection with Tourette syndrome. When an infection such as strep attacks the body, the body produces antibodies that fight the infection. If the antibodies malfunction and attack healthy cells, an autoimmune reaction occurs. Though not specified, some experts believe other types of infections may trigger Tourette's tics as well.

Although all of the causes of TS have yet to be determined, researchers are uncovering possibilities. As mentioned earlier in conjunction with the SLITRK1 gene, researchers have identified a connection with the basal ganglia, a part of the brain. The basal ganglia are a cluster of nerve cells that affect the function of smooth muscle tissue, facilitated by the neurotransmitters acetylcholine and dopamine. Smooth muscle tissue controls involuntary muscle movements. With Tourette syndrome, these nerve cells appear to produce an excess of dopamine. Dopamine helps regulate normal functioning of the central nervous system, including movement and emotions. Too much of this neurotransmitter can cause hypersensitivity, which, in turn, causes involuntary movement.

According to some research, including that of the Addiction Research Foundation in Toronto, Ontario, Canada, another neurotransmitter, serotonin, may also be involved in triggering TS tics. Although most of the serotonin in the body occurs in the intestine and regulates intestinal movement, some of this chemical is also involved in the functioning of the central nervous system, affecting appetite, mood, and pain perception.

Other factors that do not directly cause TS may, nevertheless, affect its severity. Some experts believe that risky prenatal activities, such as if a mother who carries the gene smokes, drinks, uses drugs, or is exposed to toxic substances during pregnancy, could result in the child developing more severe TS symptoms. Different types of stress may also have the potential to worsen symptoms in TS sufferers. These stress factors include the breakup of a long-term relationship, such as a divorce; trouble on the job or at school; the death of a loved one; and other life-altering events.

Despite research efforts, much about the causes and traits of Tourette syndrome remains a mystery. Why do stressful events trigger tic episodes in some TS patients but not others? And why might a parent who grew up experiencing tics from TS have one child who develops the tics and another who does not? Additionally, because of the variety of the types of symptoms involved, an accurate diagnosis may take years; some people may live their entire lives dealing with an undiagnosed, mystifying condition.

One sympathetic doctor describes the mysteries of Tourette syndrome this way: "Having Tourette's is kind of like a riddle. Tourette Syndrome can be tough to understand and solve, however, like a riddle, quite easy to accept once you understand it."[5]

CHAPTER TWO

Diagnosis and Treatment

As with any illness or disorder, an early diagnosis of Tourette syndrome (TS) is vitally important to the welfare of the patient. In the case of TS, early diagnosis and treatment can help family, friends, teachers, and classmates understand that the bizarre and sometimes disruptive behaviors are beyond the person's control. This, in turn, can help prevent the person with TS from feeling like a social misfit or troublemaker because the tics are mistaken for inappropriate behavior.

An accurate diagnosis requires cooperative effort between the family and medical professionals. The diagnostic process for TS differs from approaches to diagnosing most medical conditions because some of the testing procedures are physical and others are psychological. As with the testing procedures, treatment programs are also varied. They can involve a combination of medications and psychotherapy, depending on the severity of the condition.

The Tourette Syndrome Spectrum

For the purpose of diagnosis and treatment, TS is divided into three general classifications. These classifications carry varying degrees of severity. The first type, known as pure Tourette syndrome, accounts for about 40 percent of all diagnosed cases and is not associated with any other disorder or condition. This type is sometimes so mild that it remains undiagnosed. If the person has any vocal or motor tics, they may be overlooked as allergies or as simple behavioral quirks. In fact, some people may never know they have TS.

The second type is called full-blown Tourette syndrome. People with full-blown Tourette syndrome experience two or more different kinds of tics. These may include more extreme types of tics, such as coprolalia, echolalia, or other types of disruptive or violent tics.

The third type, Tourette syndrome plus, is a comorbid disorder. This means that, in addition to Tourette syndrome, the person has other disorders. The disorder most frequently associated with Tourette syndrome plus is obsessive-compulsive disorder (OCD). In fact, OCD has been associated with anywhere from 20 to 60 percent of diagnosed cases of Tourette syndrome plus, depending on the study.

As the name suggests, obsessions and compulsions affect the behavior of people with OCD. Obsessions are persistent impulses, thoughts, or mental images that cause the person to feel anxious and stressed. Compulsions are repeated behaviors, such as constantly checking light switches, repeatedly washing hands, hoarding and saving, mentally repeating words over and over, or counting rituals. People with OCD believe that something bad will happen if they do not perform these tasks, although there is absolutely nothing about this ritualistic behavior that can actually prevent something bad from happening or cause something good to happen. Being troubled by OCD behaviors in addition to tics can be particularly embarrassing and troublesome for anyone, but especially for young people.

Author Amy S. Wilensky, who has TS with OCD, recalls an embarrassing experience some years ago in a school gym class when she became "stuck" in a behavior, compelled to bounce a basketball while chanting a phrase in her head:

> I may have kept bouncing until I dropped from exhaustion, wore size 2 shoe grooves into the hard scruffed floor

Obsessive compulsive disorder is often associated with Tourette syndrome plus. OCD impulses may include the need to organize or label things a certain way or to repeatedly wash one's hands.

of the gym, but the shrill whistle just inches from my ear breaks the rhythm, the pattern, the words, and the ball rolls off into a corner, hits the wall by a lunch bench locked up for later, when the gym will turn back into the cafeteria. I look around at my classmates, a few of whom stare back at me openly with puzzlement that mirrors my own.

"What's wrong with you?" The gym teacher shouts, crouching so his face is level with mine and the background closes in and the voices grow louder and I am in gym class, it's winter, we're inside, we're shooting baskets again.[6]

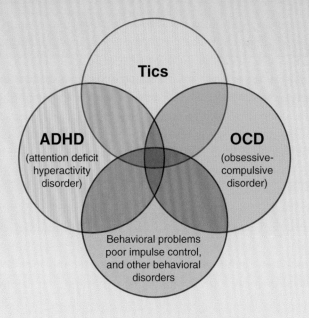

Clinical Elements of Tourette Syndrome

Tourette syndrome is a comorbid disorder that is often accompanied by other disorders such as ADHD and OCD.

Tics

ADHD
(attention deficit hyperactivity disorder)

OCD
(obsessive-compulsive disorder)

Behavioral problems poor impulse control, and other behavioral disorders

Taken from: *New England Journal of Medicine* 2001;345:1184–1192.

Diagnoses of depression and anxiety can also be tied to Tourette syndrome plus. Depression, in this instance, does not mean occasionally feeling down or blue as most people do from time to time. Clinical depression is much more serious. It can cause mood swings, problems with appetite, and in extreme cases, thoughts of suicide. This type of depression can cause sleep problems as well.

In rare instances, conduct disorders can be associated with Tourette syndrome plus. The behaviors associated with conduct disorders are sometimes so potentially dangerous or violent that they can lead to serious trouble, even arrest and jail time. Two of these are vandalism and pyromania; the latter of which is a fascination with fire that can include starting fires and watching them burn. Other behaviors include ditching school, fighting, cruelty to animals, stealing, and habitual lying.

If people with any of these severe symptoms do not receive diagnosis and help, this disorder can seriously disrupt their lives. It can damage work and school performance, harm friendships, and place an enormous strain on families.

Diagnosing Tourette Syndrome

Although Tourette syndrome cannot be cured, its symptoms can be addressed, enabling TS sufferers to live happy, productive lives. Success lies in early diagnosis and treatment. For the most accurate diagnosis, parents need the services of appropriate care professionals. For instance, if parents suspect their child may have TS, they can research psychologists or neurologists who have experience treating patients with TS. Because large cities tend to have more specialized medical resources than smaller towns, such a location would be the best place to begin the search. The American Board of Psychiatry and Neurology or the American Board of Medical Specialists can verify the professional credentials of any specialists the family may be considering. Additionally, the National Tourette Syndrome Association can often refer patients to the nearest experts in this field, though they do not make specific recommendations. Local branches of these organizations can be located by telephone or Internet.

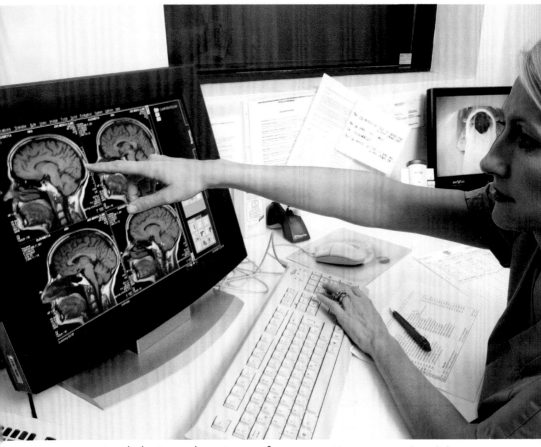

A radiologist analyzes images from magnetic resonance imagining, or MRI. This test may help doctors diagnose Tourette syndrome.

Because of the many kinds of tics connected with TS and the range of severity from very mild and hardly noticeable to bizarre and sometimes violent, TS can go undiagnosed or be misdiagnosed. Additionally, there are currently no screening tests, like blood tests or neurological tests, designed specifically to diagnose the disorder. This being the case, a doctor's first effort may focus on a family history of parents, grandparents, and other relatives who have experienced similar symptoms as well as a journal of the patient's own symptoms. This information includes the age at which tics were first noticed and what kinds of tics the patient first experienced, such as eye blinking, sniffling, or throat clearing. Information about any subsequent tics the patient developed is also included, detailing their frequency, severity, and the conditions under which the tics occurred. If the patient is an adult, he or she should maintain a personal record of tics to present to the physician in charge of his or her diagnosis.

In order to diagnose TS, health professionals look for several specific signs. For instance, *The Diagnostic and Statistical Manual of Mental Disorders* provides a symptoms checklist that can serve as a guide when diagnosing Tourette syndrome:

1. Both multiple motor and one or more vocal tics have been present at some time during the illness, although not necessarily concurrently. (A tic is a sudden, rapid, recurrent, non-rhythmic stereotyped motor movement or vocalization.)

2. The tics occur many times a day (usually in bouts) nearly every day or intermittently throughout a period of more than one year, and during this period there was never a tic-free period of more than three consecutive months.

3. The disturbance causes marked distress or significant impairment in social, occupational, or other important areas of functioning.

4. The onset is before 18 years.

5. The disturbance is not due to the direct physiological effects of a substance (e.g., Huntington's Disease or post-viral encephalitis.)[7]

There is, however, some professional disagreement concerning this checklist. Some experts argue that certain types of tics vary from this description. Furthermore, some people diagnosed with Tourette syndrome experience tic-free periods far longer than three months. Additionally, the term *marked distress* does not necessarily apply to all TS patients. Many adults and children who have TS maintain full, rewarding lives

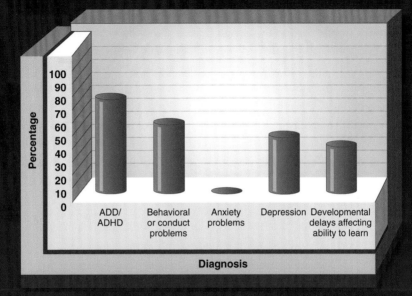

Tourette Syndrome Diagnosed in Persons Aged 6–17 in the United States

Notes: The figure above shows the prevalence of selected diagnoses among persons aged 6–17 years who have ever received a diagnosis of Tourette syndrome by parent report in the United States in 2007. Among children ever diagnosed with TS, 79% also had been diagnosed with at least one co-occurring mental health or neurodevelopmental condition. Sixty-four percent had been diagnosed with ADHD, 43% with behavioral or conduct problems, 0% with anxiety problems, 36% with depression, and 28% with a developmental delay affecting the child's ability to learn.

Taken from: MMWR © 2009 Centers for Disease Control and Prevention (CDC).

despite the condition. Regardless of these discrepancies, this checklist remains a useful starting point for parents beginning to seek help for their children as well as for adults whose symptoms closely match the five-item criteria.

Although no test exists for the single purpose of diagnosing Tourette syndrome, physicians may request some tests in order to rule out other conditions that can also cause tics or bizarre behavior, such as some kinds of brain tumors. One such device, an electroencephalogram, records electrical activity in the brain. A computed tomography scan is another available test.

With a computer image cross section, this device can create a three-dimensional image of the brain. Finally, physicians may order a magnetic resonance imaging scan (MRI), which can create sectional images of soft tissues inside the body.

Because OCD and ADHD sometimes occur in conjunction with Tourette syndrome, physicians may evaluate potential TS patients for these disorders as well. For the overall welfare of the patient, these associated conditions also require attention and treatment. Many testing instruments are available to evaluate these disorders. For instance, the University of Hamburg in Germany has one such test: a questionnaire composed of twenty-

The *Diagnostic and Statistical Manual of Mental Disorders* provides a checklist that may guide a diagnosis of Tourette's.

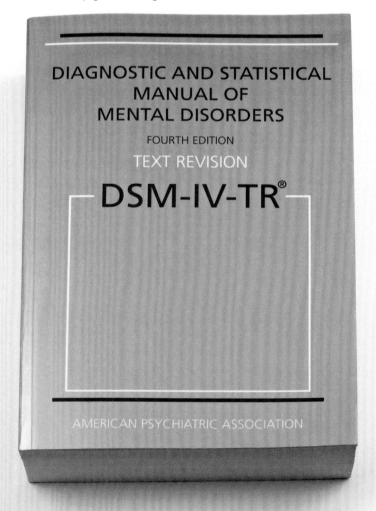

Comorbid Conditions

On its own, Tourette syndrome can bring major challenges to a person's life, but when TS occurs in conjunction with other conditions, the challenges can multiply. Attention deficit/hyperactivity disorder (ADHD) and obsessive-compulsive disorder (OCD) are conditions that commonly occur with Tourette syndrome plus.

ADHD is a common childhood disorder. The three subtypes of ADHD are predominantly hyperactive-impulsive, predominantly inattentive, and combined hyperactive-impulsive and inattentive. Children who have symptoms of inattention are easily distracted, become easily bored after a few minutes with an activity, have trouble completing assignments, have trouble processing information, and have difficulty following instructions. Hyperactivity symptoms include fidgeting, being in constant motion, running about aimlessly, and having trouble being still for any period of time. Impulsivity includes impatience, interrupting others, and poor control of emotions.

OCD is one of the most common anxiety disorders. As its name implies, it is characterized by obsessions and compulsions. Some common obsessions are aggressive impulses, sexual thoughts, needing things to be orderly and symmetrical, and fear of germs and dirt. Compulsions drive people with OCD to perform rituals tied to their obsessions, such as fear of germs and dirt, compelling a person to wash his or her hands repeatedly, to the point of chaffing the skin. Another obsession involves turning off lights, compelling a person to go from room to room repeatedly checking the lights.

Although dealing with the symptoms of TS is a daunting task on its own, symptoms such as ritualistic or out-of-control behavior should not be overlooked as childhood quirks or phases. Left untreated, ADHD or OCD can cause life-long problems.

seven true and false questions to evaluate people for OCD. The questions address troubling but less critical obsessions, such as hand-washing rituals, the compelling urge to perform tasks a certain number of times, and counting rituals, as well as dangerous obsessions, such as self-injury and thoughts of suicide. The National Institute of Mental Health has a similar questionnaire for OCD, composed of twenty yes-and-no questions.

Other questionnaires and testing instruments also address ADHD. One of these, called ACTeRS, focuses on four factors: hyperactivity, oppositional behavior (arguing with adults, ignoring rules, annoying people, and experiencing tantrums), attention span, and social skills. This instrument is designed for students from kindergarten to eighth grade. The Brown Attention Deficit Disorder Scales is a quick-screening process composed of forty items. These items focus on six areas: ability to sustain attention, ability to regulate moods, recall of learned material, ability to activate and organize work tasks, the ability to remain focused to complete tasks, and short-term memory. A third instrument is the Copeland Symptoms Checklist for Attention Deficit Disorders. Like the other testing instruments, the purpose of this evaluation is to determine whether a young person has the symptoms of ADHD. The areas addressed in this test include cognitive and visual-motor achievement, relationships with peers, level of distractibility, impulsive behavior, emotional issues, family relationships, attention-seeking behavior, overall maturity, and how well the child complies with directions and rules.

With the need for so many different kinds of tests, some to rule out other conditions as well as others to evaluate associated disorders, diagnosing Tourette syndrome can be a very frustrating and time-consuming experience for patients and their families.

Conventional Treatments

Although at this time there is no cure for Tourette syndrome, once an accurate diagnosis is made, health professionals will work with the patient and family to determine the best way to treat that person's condition. If the person's symptoms are very mild or he or she is coping well, the best response may be no

Serotonin

Melatonin

This diagram illustrates the neurotransmitter serotonin during a chemical synapse in a cell. Serotonin may contribute to tic behavior in a Tourette's patient, as well as to OCD.

treatment at all. However, if the disorder is impacting the patient's daily life, a number of treatment options are available to help the patient manage the symptoms.

One approach to treatment is medication. Certain medications can help improve attention while decreasing tics, OCD symptoms, and hyperactivity and impulsivity. As with any type of treatment, however, there are both positive and negative issues associated with medications. First, many medications do not immediately stop or lessen the severity of tics. Some medications have to build up in the body over a period of days or even weeks before they begin to work. Additionally, if a patient needs to come off of a medication, many drugs cannot be discontinued all at once. If some medications are stopped suddenly, the patient may experience a rebound, meaning a period of very severe tic symptoms. In fact, for a time the tics could be worse than they were before the patient began treatment. For the welfare of the patient, medications must be "stepped down," or gradually decreased, before they are stopped completely.

Antihypertensive Drugs

Several medications can reduce tic symptoms in people with mild to moderate tics. Two of these medications are antihypertensive drugs sometimes used in the treatment of high blood pressure, clondine (Catapres) and guanfacine (Tenex.) These drugs limit the amount of norepinephrine—a neurotransmitter that can increase heart rate—that is released in the body by the neurons, or nerve cells, located in the brain and other parts of the central nervous system. Norepinephrine, in turn, limits the amount of dopamine released in the body. Less dopamine can reduce the effects of tics.

These antihypertensive drugs can have side effects, however, such as sleepiness and lightheadedness. They can also cause dry mouth, irritability, depression, and, in some instances, skin rashes. Nonetheless, careful administration of these drugs can greatly reduce the chances of such side effects.

Two of the drugs used to treat moderate to severe tics are the neuroleptics known as risperidone (Risperadal) and haloperidol (Haldol.) Neuroleptics are tranquilizers sometimes used to treat mental conditions such as severe depression, paranoia, and schizophrenia, a mental condition characterized by hallucinations and delusions. Although side effects with neuroleptics are rare, patients taking these drugs should be carefully monitored. Possible side effects include weight gain and phobia, an unnatural fear of objects or people. Other potential side effects are involuntary movements of the mouth and tongue and jerky movements of the arms or legs. The latter symptoms are more likely to occur in patients with mental retardation.

Atypical neuroleptics are the third type of medications used to treat some cases of Tourette syndrome. In addition to blocking dopamine, atypical neuroleptics also block the neurotransmitter serotonin. Serotonin is believed to be one contributing factor in tic activity and may also contribute to OCD symptoms, a double threat to people with Tourette syndrome plus with OCD.

One widely studied atypical neuroleptic is risperidone (Risperadal.) Many experts believe that this medication may reduce tic activity anywhere from 20 to 60 percent. As an additional benefit, risperidone may also reduce impulsive behavior and outbursts of rage. Possible side effects to this drug include moderate weight gain, sleepiness, and a rapid heartbeat.

A number of other drugs that were initially developed for other uses may also be helpful in treating some TS cases. One of these drugs is Aricept, a drug used to treat the memory problems associated with Alzheimer's disease and senile dementia. This drug works by increasing the production of the neurotransmitter acetylcholine, which appears to counter the effects of excessive dopamine production.

Side Effects

Although these drugs are successful in treating many TS patients, some people fear the range of possible side effects. Author Lowell Handler, who has Tourette syndrome, describes his personal experience with side effects from the drug Haldol:

> Once Haldol was prescribed for me, I immediately felt relief from my tics. During the first two or three weeks of taking the medication I was elated by this newfound normalcy and the feeling of "fitting in." But Haldol, like any drug, has potentially dangerous short- and long-term side effects, to which I was not immediately alerted. Within two or three weeks of taking the drug, I was plagued by a gnawing hunger and mental dulling. At times I'd have fidgety restlessness, and then I'd experience the reverse—a zombielike state of lethargy and depression.[8]

Although these side effects do sometimes occur, medical professionals make every effort to provide their patients with the best information available. Before considering or choosing any possible drugs for treatment, doctors and therapists will meet with the patient and/or the patient's parents to discuss all possible treatment options and determine the best approach for that particular patient. The best course of treatment chosen for the patient might consist of a single treatment or a combination of treatment options. For instance, drug therapy may be prescribed on its own or with some sort of psychotherapy, or psychotherapy alone.

Psychobehavioral Therapies

Psychobehavioral therapies are a group of "talk" therapies. One of these, cognitive-behavioral therapy (CBT), is a system of talk therapy in which a therapist works with the patient to identify and discuss irrational thoughts and beliefs. Although it cannot stop the tics, this type of therapy can help people deal with the OCD symptoms and anxiety often associated with more severe cases of Tourette syndrome.

Like other types of talk therapies, CBT can be conducted in several ways. Sessions can be one-on-one, between the therapist and a single patient. Sessions can also be conducted in group settings, with one therapist working with several patients at the same time. A third approach is computerized CBT. In computerized CBT, the patient interacts with a computer rather than directly with a therapist. Computerized CBT is especially effective in places where actual therapists are not available or with people who do not feel comfortable speaking in person with therapists about their feelings.

CBT is based on a very practical concept. If a person can change behavior, that person can also change potentially harmful thoughts and feelings. Patients do this by learning to think differently and then putting the new thought patterns into practice. CBT generally produces fast results. Unlike other forms of talk therapy, which may continue for years, the average number of sessions for CBT is about sixteen. This type of therapy tends to work well with children and with people with some kinds of mental illness. This is because patients are actually physically involved in the process, which can give them a sense of empowerment. They also do homework assignments after sessions. It is not simply a matter of sitting and talking.

Desensitizing is one type of homework. The term *desensitizing* means repeated exposure to a situation or object that causes a person an irrational level of fear, anxiety, or stress, emotions that can trigger tics. Repeated exposure helps the person overcome the fear or anxiety associated with the object or situation. This can occur gradually, in small steps, and increase until the patient overcomes the emotional reaction. For instance, some people are irrationally fearful of escalators. To desensitize a patient, a therapist might assign him or her the task of stepping onto an immobile escalator and walking up or down the steps. The patient's next assignment might be to ride the escalator one way during a quiet time of day. After several trips, the patient would ride the escalator alone. These assignments would be fulfilled over a period of several weeks.

The therapist may also help the patient learn not to "awfulize" situations. This means imagining irrationally bad outcomes for normal, routine activities, like fearing he or she will have a sudden bout of tics while walking to the front of the classroom to make a presentation. There is a chance it could happen, but a larger chance that it will not.

Another coping skill that therapists teach patients as a part of CBT is thought blocking. Thought blocking means learning to replace thoughts that cause anxiety or stress with pleasant thoughts, thus decreasing chances of a tic episode. For instance, if a patient has an irrational fear of crowds and has to attend a student assembly, he or she can learn to replace the fear of feeling trapped in a crowded place with thoughts of a pleasant setting, such as sitting by a cool mountain stream, reading a good book or relaxing at home, or watching a favorite television program.

Like other forms of therapy, CBT is not without controversy. Whereas some therapists believe CBT is superior to other forms of talk therapy, other professionals believe that, when compared to other types of psychotherapy, it may be equally effective but not necessarily superior. This may be the case because it tends to be a shorter duration therapy and is used in

Family support for a member with Tourette's is an important form of therapy that can help reverse habits.

the treatment of a wide variety of disorders. Some experts believe that CBT receives more attention than other types of psychotherapy and if psychiatric research funding is focused on CBT, other forms of psychotherapy that may be as effective or possibly more beneficial to the patient might be overlooked.

Other less familiar forms of therapy are also available for TS patients. Habit reversal has proven successful in treating more difficult tic/compulsions, such as tics that can be physically harmful to the patient and others. Habit reversal has four components: awareness training, competing response training, motivational strategies, and social support. Awareness training is learning to become aware of stress, anxiety, or other emotions that precede a tic episode. Competing response training consists of learning stress reduction techniques, such as breathing slowly or training the body to release stress using some less noticeable movement. As part of the motivational strategies, the patient chooses rewards to receive once he or she successfully employs stress reduction techniques. Finally, social support is the family component. Family members remind the patient to use the competing responses and provide praise and support when the patient does so.

Patients must remember, though, that psychotherapy is not a "quick fix." Results from these therapies may not be seen for weeks or months, and what works for one patient may not work for another. Patients and their families must be willing to wait and work toward results.

Alternative and Complementary Therapies

Alternative therapies are therapies used in place of conventional treatments. Complementary therapies, on the other hand, are used in conjunction with conventional therapies. The usefulness of these therapies can be hard to define because information about alternative therapies usually travels informally by word of mouth, rather than as press releases provided as a result of clinical trials and other scientific research. Conventional therapies, on the other hand, are supported by the results of scientific research and field trials, groups of patients participating in drug and other types of therapeutic testing.

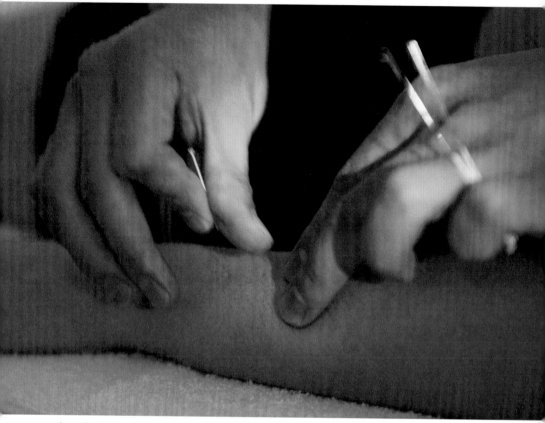

A patient receives acupuncture. This ancient therapy is commonly used in China to treat people with Tourette's.

As with conventional therapies, the patient's primary care physician should be consulted before any alternative or complementary therapies are attempted. For instance, certain types of herbal supplements may react adversely with some conventional medications prescribed for Tourette syndrome. This could make the patient sick or possibly prevent the conventional medication from working properly. The primary care physician should know if an herbal or vitamin supplement is safe to take with the medications that have been prescribed for the patient.

One reliable source to consult when considering an alternative therapy is the National Center for Complementary and

Ayurveda: An Alternative Treatment for Tourette Syndrome

Ayurvedics, a holistic approach to medicine, has been used in India and Sri Lanka for centuries. This ancient medical concept addresses both mind and body. According to ayurvedic beliefs, to achieve optimal health certain related body functions must be in balance. These include metabolism, digestion, and excretion. Any of these being out of balance can result in poor health.

Although some experts believe this holistic approach to medicine is free of side effects, others are concerned that some of the herbal preparations used in ayurvedics contain traces of poisonous heavy metals, such as mercury and arsenic. However, many ayurvedic practitioners say that the preparation of these herbal supplements filters out any such harmful substances. One ayurvedic herb used in the treatment of TS is turmeric. Called the spice of life, turmeric is a member of the ginger family. This substance is said to be successful in treating conditions that cause brain inflammation and other malfunctions of the brain.

Although this medical concept is mostly linked to India and Sri Lanka, it is gaining interest in the West. The National Institute of Ayurvedic Medicine was established in 1982 by physician Scott Gerson. The institute has a Web site, http://niam .com/corp-web/index.htm, which provides information about ayurvedics and practitioners.

The spice turmeric is an ayurvedic herb used to treat Tourette syndrome. Turmeric is thought to be an anti-inflammatory.

Alternative Medicine (NCCAM). This organization conducts and supports research into complementary and alternative therapies. The NCCAM Web site provides information about complementary and alternative medicine (CAM) therapies and nutritional supplements as well as warnings about questionable treatments.

Acupuncture is one of the oldest CAM therapies. An ancient Chinese therapy, acupuncture is based on chi, the energy force that is supposed to travel through the human body. Acupuncturists believe that if the chi gets blocked, the person becomes ill. Acupuncture treatment consists of inserting thin needles into specific points in the skin to unblock the flow. This treatment is commonly used in China for people with Tourette syndrome as well as other conditions. In fact, acupuncturists in China who participated in a study about using acupuncture to treat TS claim a success rate of nearly 75 percent, according to lead author Wu Lianzhong, who is affiliated with the acupuncture department of Tianjin College of Traditional Chinese Medicine. However, such information as tic severity and follow-up data about the patients was not included in the study material that was released for publication.

People with severe tics who suffer from joint and muscle pain may seek the services of chiropractors. Chiropractors use manipulation to make aligning adjustments along the spine and other parts of the body. According to one single case study, an adult with Tourette syndrome reported less severe symptoms during a three-month chiropractic treatment period.

As with any treatments, the credentials of CAM practitioners should be carefully researched before engaging their services.

CHAPTER THREE

Personal Challenges and Family

Like many illnesses and disorders, Tourette syndrome affects not only the person with the disorder but also his or her entire family. The individual with TS may have feelings of inferiority and guilt related to the condition and its impact on his or her family. Parents may feel they have failed in some way because they cannot "fix" their child. Siblings may feel overlooked because parents have to focus so much time and energy on the child with TS. The whole family may feel isolated because of having to forego family outings enjoyed by other families, fearing the child with TS might suddenly experience a bout of tics and cause a disruption in a restaurant, movie theater, or park.

Growing Up with Tourette Syndrome

Although Tourette syndrome is not a fatal disease and does not impact a person's life span or intelligence, it can severely impact the quality of life of the person who has it. This is true not only for people who experience extreme tics but also for those who have relatively mild ones. For instance, if children who have TS are teased at school or in any public setting because of the tics, their self-esteem can be damaged. This can cause children to emotionally withdraw, become depressed, or feel extremely insecure when at school or other places among a lot of people.

Children tease a girl outside of school. Children with Tourette syndrome may be teased because of tics and other behavior.

Tourette syndrome can have a negative effect on children at home as well. A child with TS may experience resentment from siblings, who may think he or she is receiving special treatment due to the disorder. Additionally, the child with TS may feel guilty if the family has to miss outings, like going to movies or sporting events, because the parents fear the child could have tic episodes in public.

Parents

Parents of children with Tourette syndrome are in a particularly stressful position for a variety of reasons. They may spend months or even years searching for reasons for their child's bizarre behavior. This can be a very frustrating process. It is natural for parents to want to fix their children's problems quickly, and they may feel helpless if they cannot find some way to help rid their child of something as troubling as these strange outbursts. As they go through the long, frustrating process of seeking help for their child, they are sometimes blamed for the child's behavior. They may even accept the blame, believing they have been doing something wrong as parents to cause their child to misbehave.

After their child is diagnosed with Tourette syndrome, parents are often faced with a new set of worries and emotions. At first they may be relieved to finally have a diagnosis, but if they have never heard of TS, they may be confused and bewildered by this diagnosis, not sure if finally having a diagnosis is good news or bad news. If they have previously heard of TS, they may envision the types of tics they have seen portrayed on television and in motion pictures. These are probably the coprolalia tics—the tics that involve cursing—or the nonobscene socially inappropriate tics that are outbursts of inappropriate words or phrases. They may fear that their child may one day experience these bizarre and disruptive behaviors as well. Early on in the diagnostics process, parents may not know that these kinds of tics are the rarest.

Sometimes parents want to assign guilt. This means they look for someone or something to blame for the condition. They may begin searching through family information and learn that a member of the father's or the mother's family had Tourette syndrome. One parent may try to blame the other for not knowing or, even worse, accuse the other of hiding that information. A mother or a father may try to take on personal guilt as well. Perhaps they had punished the child, believing that the tics were just out-of-control behavior, or felt shame over the child's behavior when a bout of tics occurred in a public place. One of the first issues parents need to understand during the diagnostics process is that they are not responsible for their child's TS.

Parents may also experience sadness or depression, believing their child might never have a "normal" life. They may resent seeing families enjoying public outings together, thinking they will never again be able to enjoy family activities together. They may also feel angry or resentful toward other parents when they brag about their children or talk about their fun times together.

When a child is diagnosed with TS, his or her parents must begin their personal education. Yet the material available can be overwhelming, and some of it is conflicting. To better understand the information, parents need to review it in small sections, one book or article at a time, rather than trying to take in everything at once. One important fact parents need to know is that there is no way to predict which types of tics their child will experience or their frequency. Parents will learn that Tourette syndrome is a waxing and waning disorder. This means that their child may experience periods during which the tics occur frequently and other times when he or she has few, if any, tics.

Additionally, parents have the difficult job of learning to differentiate between tic behavior and inappropriate behavior because not all inappropriate behavior can necessarily be blamed on the tics. Despite any medical diagnosis a child receives, parents are still responsible for setting boundaries for their children. Parents need to be aware of age-appropriate behavior for their children and to act on misbehavior accordingly. If a child experiences violent outbursts that are related to TS, parents must protect their other children and the property of the other children. Siblings should not feel victimized or be expected to accept abusive treatment or damage to their belongings because of the disorder.

One way parents can help curb inappropriate behavior is by using positive reinforcement techniques to focus on the child's appropriate behavior. Author Karen Bearss of the Yale Child Study Center had this to say about positive reinforcement: "This can take the form of 'special time' where the parent and child participate in a mutually enjoyable activity. This also can mean attending to and rewarding specific appropriate behaviors."[9]

Parents of children with Tourette's go through a variety of emotions, including guilt, shame, and frustration over their child's diagnosis.

Likewise, it is important for parents to be good role models for their child with Tourette syndrome. Children learn emotional responses and other behaviors from their parents. Thus, parents need to control their personal feelings in the presence of their child and maintain an even emotional state. If the child sees a parent acting distressed, depressed, or anxious, he or she will become anxious as well. If, on the other hand, parents maintain calm, positive attitudes about their child's condition, the child will tend to be more relaxed and positive about the condition too.

A Teen Helping Teens and TS

Now eighteen years old, Jennifer Zwilling was seven when she was diagnosed with Tourette syndrome. She had gotten into trouble for rolling her eyes at something a teacher said, and the teacher became angry. This was because the teacher did not understand TS and its symptoms. Instead of becoming shy and withdrawn over her condition, Jennifer began speaking about TS to teachers and students in her school, educating them about the many types of tics that are involuntary symptoms of the condition, not behavior issues.

In 2007 Zwilling was one of the winners of the BRICK Award (now called the Do Something Award). Do Something is a Manhattan-based nonprofit organization. Recipients of this award are teens who are making outstanding contributions in health, environmental, and social issues. In addition to receiving a community grant award of ten thousand dollars, recipients' photographs appear on bags of chips, such as Doritos.

Zwilling has trained more than a hundred volunteers to carry the TS message; however, she also continues to give presentations herself. To help people understand what it is like to function with TS, she conducts an exercise. She has the students write the Pledge of Allegiance, which normally takes a couple of minutes at most. As they write, though, they are instructed to erase every third word

and rewrite it, and to touch the floor every time Zwilling claps her hands. According to Zwilling, no one has ever finished this exercise.

This young New Yorker has inspired a new generation to learn about TS and be courteous to those who have the condition.

Jennifer Zwilling speaks at a presentation before the Tourette Syndrome Association.

Burn out is another serious issue among parents of children with Tourette syndrome. Parents sometimes need to step back from the reading and research and simply engage in normal activities. It is important to continue participating in social activities, hobbies, and exercise. Parents are more effective participants in the welfare of their children if they maintain their own physical and mental well-being.

Additionally, one family's experiences with TS may be completely different from those of another family. Each family has its own unique experiences. Efforts that are successful for one family may not be successful for another. Because of this, the adjustment process may be a trial-and-error experience for parents. Parents are not failing their children if some technique that has worked for another child does not work for their child. If one effort fails, the parents can simply move on and try something else.

Siblings and Friends

Being the brother or sister of a person with a disorder or a disease can be a very stressful experience. Sometimes the sibling without the condition feels ignored and unappreciated. Parents have to spend a lot of time and effort on the sibling with the problem, and that means they have less time and attention to give to the other children in the family. The other children may think this is unfair. They may feel left out and believe their parents do not care as much for them as they do for the brother or sister with the condition. For instance, it may appear that the sibling with TS always gets his or her way with the parents and can do anything he or she likes. It can be very difficult not to feel resentful toward that brother or sister when it seems like he or she is always the center of attention, or not to feel embarrassed when the sibling experiences tics while the family is out somewhere together.

In the book *Views from Our Shoes: Growing Up with a Brother or Sister with Special Needs,* an eleven-year-old girl discusses the challenges and issues of growing up with a brother who has TS and how her mother helped her understand:

My brother has Tourette's Syndrome and says bad words that he can't control. Sometimes I feel it's unfair because there are times I wish I could say what he says! . . . Mom took him to the doctors and came home and explained to me that he couldn't stop the weird noises that he makes. I understood more about it when she showed me a video-tape about it.[10]

If the sibling with Tourette syndrome attends the same school as the other siblings, this can cause an entirely differ-ent set of problems for the other children in the family. If some-one bullies or makes fun of their sibling, they may try to fight the other students to defend their brother or sister. The sib-lings in the family who do not have TS may be teased and taunted as well. This can lead them to isolate themselves from classmates and other people outside their family and avoid hobbies and activities they once enjoyed.

Siblings of children with TS may also try to be the "perfect" child. They may try to "make up" for the sibling with the disor-der by trying to do everything flawlessly, like making perfect grades in school. They may take on extra responsibilities at home and not go to their parents when they have problems of their own because they do not want to put added burdens on their parents. Basically, they give up childhood, assuming adult roles far too early.

On the other hand, some siblings may respond by acting out because they see this as a way of getting attention too. Some siblings, however, might emotionally withdraw from the fam-ily, choosing to stay in their own rooms and avoid confronta-tions with the sibling with TS; meanwhile, older brothers and sisters may avoid coming home by spending their extra time in the library, at the mall, or at the movies, or they may choose to spend their afternoons in the homes of friends who have "nor-mal" families.

If a brother or sister has Tourette syndrome, the other sib-lings can help themselves by learning what the disorder is, how it affects people, and what they can do to help their sibling. For instance, they can learn why their sibling can sometimes

Two friends with Tourette's share the challenges of living with the disease. Support from siblings and friends is very important.

suppress the tics, but cannot do it all of the time. They can also learn why a sibling's sometimes violent behavior, directed at them or their parents, may also be a symptom of the disability rather than a deliberate act of violence. This might help them be less embarrassed or resentful when a tic occurs in public or more inclined to try to explain the disorder to their peers rather than getting into fights or feeling resentful toward others.

Coping Every Day

The whole issue of coping means different things to different members of the family. For the person with Tourette syndrome, it is the day-to-day coping with something over which he or she has little or no control: the tics. Some people are able to maintain positive attitudes. They are so used to having the tics that they see no particular problem with them. It is just one part of their lives. They may take the attitude that other people's reactions to their tics are the other people's problems. However, some people with TS are very self-conscious about their tics. They may withdraw into themselves, avoiding public places and activities.

For the children who tend to become withdrawn and avoid family outings, parents can do several things to avoid or cut down on embarrassing situations. On one extreme, instead of isolating the family and never going out together, or, the other end of the spectrum, ignoring the issue of public disruption that some tics can cause, the parents can make some modifications. For instance, if the family likes to go to movies or the theater, parents can request aisle seats near exits. This way, if the child goes into a noisy bout of tics, the parents can quickly remove the child from the auditorium.

One young man whose TS followed him into adulthood describes the ways he copes with the tics:

> Every day is a challenge but there are mechanisms I've adopted in order to cope with the condition. When I'm eating, I prefer to exclude myself from a group situation rather than spitting food out all over the dining table. If I

have to listen when someone's talking I find a pen or a piece of plastic and roll it about in my mouth because it gives me something to concentrate on. It suppresses my tics.[11]

Families who attend church or temple together can sometimes use this time as a testing ground for going out in public. They can explain Tourette syndrome to their family minister, priest, or rabbi, and he or she could then explain the disorder to the members of the parish or congregation. In fact, most people want to be supportive and helpful when someone in their group is dealing with a health issue or any type of personal problem.

Rather than isolate themselves, Tourette's sufferers must develop coping mechanisms to live a relatively normal life, such as choosing aisle seating at the movies.

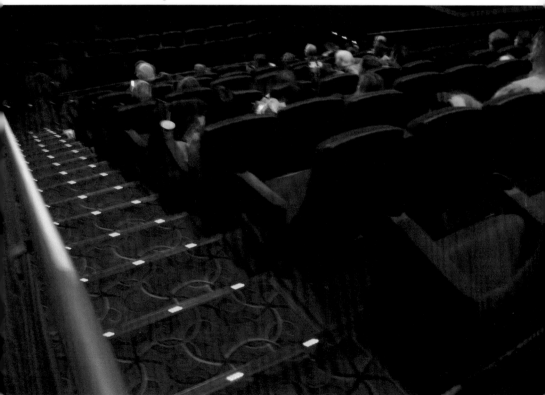

The child with TS can take an active role in the coping process as well. He or she can learn to interact with others in public in such a way that other people may focus on the person, not the tic. For instance, if a young person with TS begins to feel a tic coming on while in a store, an office, or some other public place, he or she could approach the nearest employee, briefly state the situation, and ask if there is a private place, out of the public eye, where he or she could wait until the tic passes.

Among family and friends, it is important for the person with TS to be able to speak openly about the disorder and his or her feelings about it. Sharing with trusted friends or family members is a part of the coping process. It is also important for parents to speak honestly and openly with their children about Tourette syndrome, but they must explain it to their children at age-appropriate levels. For instance, a sibling who is in high school might understand what the term *neurological disorder* means, but a nine-year-old sibling would not. However, a nine-year-old would understand that the sibling cannot help having tics any more than he or she can help coughing with a cold.

On the other hand, parents need to help the child affected with Tourette syndrome to understand that life is not perfectly fair; therefore, people will sometimes react rudely to tics. Some people may stare or point. Others might be frightened by the tics. The child needs to be prepared for these reactions and will have to learn appropriate ways to deal with them. For instance, at some point an older child may experience a bout of tics in a public place, like on a city bus, which could be very unsettling for the other passengers. This child can quietly apologize for the disruption to the nearest person and briefly explain that the tics are part of a neurological disorder. In most cases, this will lessen the general anxiety.

Finally, another excellent coping tool is a sense of humor. Humor can diffuse a lot of tension. If the person with TS can joke about it, others may feel more comfortable talking about the condition, asking questions, and responding more calmly when the person experiences tics. This can be especially helpful in gatherings of extended family and in some informal work and school settings.

Support Groups

Many people with Tourette syndrome as well as other diseases and disorders benefit from support groups. In fact, support groups are not only for the patient but also for his or her family. Information about support groups and services can be obtained from the family health care provider, school counselors, and Web sites for groups on both national and state levels.

One national organization is the National Tourette Syndrome Association. Its Web site provides support for young people as well as adults. The site provides information about current research, basic information about TS for the newly diagnosed, and links to other helpful sites. The young people's section includes a newsletter written by and for kids. There are also several success stories about people with TS in the young people's section, including athletes, writers, and even a beauty queen.

The Tourette Syndrome of Texas group is one example of a strong state-level organization. Its Web site provides information about state resources, links to national organizations, feedback opportunities, and information about an annual camp for kids called du Ballon Rouge, or Of the Red Balloon. Founded in 2003, du Ballon Rouge is a camp specifically for kids with Tourette syndrome. At the camp, these young people find an atmosphere of acceptance where they can pursue activities and experience situations they may have previously avoided or been denied because of their disorder. They do not have to worry about suppressing or hiding their symptoms, and this lessens their stress significantly. There is no need to feel shy or uncomfortable around the other campers because they experience tics as well. Faculty and staff are specifically trained to meet the needs of children with TS. In fact, some of the adult staff members also have the disorder.

New Jersey has its own Tourette syndrome support Web site. This site provides links to a number of regional support services throughout the state for both TS patients and their families. It also has a kids' support link.

Georgia recently held its first summer camp for young people with TS. The result of ten years' work on the part of

Internet Support

A number of online support sites are available for Tourette syndrome patients and their families. One of these is Tourette Syndrome Online. In addition to providing a wealth of information, the site also provides links to TS chat groups, pen pals, scholarship information, and personal accounts of people who have been affected by TS or have a family member with the condition.

Created by Craig Whitley, whose son has Tourette syndrome plus with ADHD, this site includes many useful references, including a section for frequently asked question, such as "Will my tics ever go away?" Whitley explains that for some people, the tics do disappear, but for others they remain. He also addresses the issue of the embarrassment and humiliation that can result when people experience tic episodes in public.

Through this Web site, families can obtain referral information for physicians and data about medications and other types of treatment. Families can also use this site to locate international, national, and local chapters of the Tourette Syndrome Association as well as educational information. In creating this site, Whitley has taken his family's experiences with the challenges of TS and created a valuable source of information for other families facing similar challenges.

Tourette Syndrome Online
3139 Holcombe Blvd., Suite 265
Houston, TX 77025
www.tourette-syndrome.com

teacher/author Brad Cohen, who also has TS, the camp was a weeklong experience for fifty young people from across the country. Cohen describes the purpose of the camp:

> While here at Camp Twitch and Shout we don't talk about Tourette in a formal situation. This isn't a therapy session, this isn't school. They come to the camp environment where they are around other people that are very similar

to them. All of a sudden any problem or any challenge that they've had in life disappears and they have the opportunity to be like any other child.[12]

Camps, organizations, and informal support groups are important for the family as well as for the individual with Tourette syndrome. Young people have the opportunity to meet and come to know other young people who have TS, many of whom lead active, rewarding lives. Families have the opportunity to participate in regular gatherings as well as holiday functions with other families who understand the disorder. These gatherings provide a place where no one has to be concerned about offending or upsetting anyone if a family member experiences a bout of tics. The major benefit of the support groups is to help the person with TS as well as the family to understand that they are not alone and that other people who live in the same community have many of the same concerns and challenges.

CHAPTER FOUR

Tourette Syndrome at School

Unless children with Tourette syndrome (TS) are home-schooled, they will face the daily challenges of coping with the symptoms of the disorder in the hallways and classrooms of public or private schools. These challenges involve reading, writing, and solving math problems when sometimes the body is simply not cooperating. Other challenges include possible negative reactions from some of the other students, anything from taunting and name-calling to social isolation. Any of these issues, singly, can negatively impact a child's self-esteem, but when the child is hit with several at once, it can be totally over-whelming, causing the child to have bad feelings about the school and the people there.

The Importance of Communication

Although some parents may be reluctant to approach teachers or otherwise call attention to a child's disability, fearing that their child will be treated differently, parents of students with TS have a unique opportunity to help educate the educators. Communication between parents and school is a very important factor in a child's education. This is extremely critical if the child has a disorder that could affect his or her learning or interaction with other students. If a disability is not physically apparent, such as being visually impaired or unable to walk, the people with whom the student will interact on a daily basis have no way of knowing what is going on with that person. If the student suddenly begins parroting a teacher's words, the teacher might believe the student is being deliberately rude or disrespectful. If the student suddenly begins howling or grunting in the middle of a lesson, the entire classroom could be disrupted and valuable time wasted as the teacher struggles to restore order. Additionally, this could leave the student open to ridicule.

Because of these factors and others, it is important for parents to bring the school into the loop by communicating with

Parents meet with a teacher about their child. Communication between parents, child, and teachers is very important in providing support to the student with Tourette's.

the counselors and teachers concerning their child's disorder and specific needs, such as keeping the school nurse and staff up to date regarding any medications the child takes and any side effects the medications may cause. Parents can also authorize physicians to provide the school with updates when there are changes in prescriptions or the amount of medication the student takes. Additionally, parents can supply teachers and counselors with handouts and brochures about Tourette syndrome. This is a good plan because there is always a chance that the parents may have more up-to-date materials than those of the school counselor or nurse.

One parent of a student with TS explains her efforts to keep the lines of communication open between her home and the school:

> At the beginning of each new term of school, my daughter and I would meet with the new teachers to explain TS and her accommodations. Besides listing what the teachers needed to do, we also listed my daughter's responsibilities. For example, she took [her] tests away from the classroom so the teacher had to be prepared for that. However, it was my daughter's responsibility to find a place ahead of time to take the test, perhaps in an office or another classroom during a teacher's prep time. This was good training for my daughter, helpful to the already burdened teachers, and demonstrated that we are all part of the team.[13]

By explaining to teachers and staff that their child has tics, involuntary behaviors that may appear to be behavioral problems but are, in fact, symptoms of a neurological disorder, parents can help avoid potentially serious misunderstandings. Some parents choose to allow teachers and staff to inform classmates about their child's condition in order to head off potential disruptions. In fact, some parents choose to be a part of this communication process, openly answering students' questions about TS, the different types of tics, and whether the tics will ever go away. Parents can also volunteer to act as chaperones on school outings, not only so they can be on hand should a problem occur but also to enjoy the experience with their child and the other students and observe how their child interacts with classmates.

In addition to parents sharing information about the disorder and what kinds of tics their child experiences, they can also share information about their child's specific strengths and talents. He

Teaching About Tourette Syndrome

Most young people have some knowledge of conditions such as diabetes, cancer, heart problems, hypertension, and asthma, at least in a general way. They tend to accept these as health conditions over which people have little or no control. They have been exposed to these conditions in the media and may have discussed them in school or at home in connection with family members. However, most young people have little if any knowledge of Tourette syndrome. This presents a unique teaching opportunity.

Even if no students with TS are currently enrolled on a campus, there is always a chance that students from that campus could encounter a person experiencing a bout of tics elsewhere, such as at a park, a mall, or in a movie theater. Knowledge of TS would prompt young people to react with empathy rather than fear or ridicule.

A brief, simple lesson would explain that TS occurs when a person's brain lacks the "stop signs" that prevent involuntary actions, such as grimacing, twitching, growling, or shouting. The lesson could compare bouts of tics to asthma attacks, both of which are beyond the control of the person experiencing them. The onset of a tic could also be compared to a sneeze. The person may sense that it is coming but can do nothing to prevent it. Such matter-of-fact approaches can help demystify the condition for young people.

or she might be a talented artist, athlete, or musician. By sharing this information with the teachers, the teachers can in turn be instrumental in helping build on the child's talents and skills. This way, the child is not perceived only as "the kid with TS."

Armed with knowledge of the student's neurological disorder, the needs that go along with it, as well as the student's talents and skills, teachers can become a part of the student's support team. Because the average school day is about eight hours long, including after-school activities, the school's time with the student is second only to the family's time. Teachers have the opportunity to observe the student in peer settings, away from the family's acceptance and support. Teachers see

"Tic, Tic, Tic"

A Tourette's sufferer explains what the onset of a bout of tics feels like in a way most people can understand:

Imagine speaking in front of a group of your peers. All eyes are focused on you and what you have to say. But the bottom of your foot itches and that's all you can think about. You can't itch it right now, with everyone watching, but you can't ignore it either. So you continue to speak. The more you try to ignore it, the more you are aware. Your thoughts are split between presenting your speech and thinking about ignoring the itch. It's difficult to think of both but the itch won't go away and yet, you have more to talk about. Finally, your talking ends, you run to a private place, pull off your shoe, and itch it like crazy! Ahhhh . . . relief. You held it together, the feeling had intensified and finally you could take care of it and relax.

Now try reading the paragraph above again, but this time every time a sentence ends roll your eyes, clear your throat and snap your fingers. Every time you read the word "itch," think about the way your sock feels on your foot. Go ahead, try it.

Rindy Walton, "Tic, Tic, Tic," Experiencing the Journey, March 18, 2007. http://rindy .wordpress.com/2007/03/18/tic-tic-tic.

how the student acts toward classmates, and how classmates behave toward that student. Teachers observe self-esteem issues, whether the student behaves as "one of the gang" or shies away from groups. Teachers attuned to the various nonverbal communication behaviors that students exhibit in the classroom, cafeteria, and hallways will usually know if a student is being taunted, ridiculed, bullied, or otherwise harassed, and he or she can swiftly respond to the situation and keep parents informed of any such issues. Although this extra communication adds to the teacher's already overloaded day, this extra measure of effort can help head off even more serious problems for the student with TS, such as depression, refusing to go to school, and even suicide attempts.

Friends can also be an important part of the communication loop and show support for a buddy with TS. Students say things to other students that they would not say to teachers. Some people are very cleaver at hiding harassing behavior, such as in the locker room, out of the sight of the coaches. Telling a teacher, coach, or other adult that a student is being taunted or harassed is not tattling or ratting out someone; it is being responsible and being a friend.

Finally, students who have TS have a responsibility in the communication process as well. If the student feels confident enough, he or she could do a presentation on Tourette syndrome for science class, thereby taking an active role in educating others about TS. Additionally, students with TS or any other disorder should always speak up and tell a person in authority if they are being bothered, bullied, or harassed by other students. Regular conversations with counselors or student sponsors help the teachers and staff understand what is going on in the student's life, both positive and negative. The adults in authority then can lend a hand if they are needed or simply give a few words of encouragement, which everyone, young or old, needs from time to time, whether they have a disability or not.

It Is the Law

Several laws have been enacted to protect the rights of students with physical challenges and other disabilities. These include

Section 504 of the Rehabilitation Act of 1973, the Individuals with Disabilities Act, the Americans with Disabilities Act, and other federal and state laws that deal with special education programs and the rights of the disabled. These laws benefit students with physical, neurological, and mental disabilities. Having a neurological disorder, students with Tourette syndrome are protected under such laws. The laws protect the rights and needs of students in elementary school, secondary school, and even college. A few colleges, however, may balk at these laws.

Teacher/author Brad Cohen discusses a particularly frustrating experience when he was required to take a qualifying

President George W. Bush, seated, signs the 2004 Individuals with Disabilities Education Improvement Act.

test to enter graduate school and was initially refused a private, quiet space in which to take the entrance exam: "I was angry and frustrated about the entire situation, mainly because it was so unnecessary. . . . I was completely stressed out, and for what reason? Because the people administering the test were so obstinate that they refused to give me the special accommodations that I was legally entitled to."[14]

In most schools and colleges, though, the laws are followed. These laws guarantee students with disabilities, including disorders such as Tourette syndrome, the right to a public school education that appropriately meets the student's needs. Some parts of these laws spell out exactly how long qualifying students have the right to a free public school education. For instance, handicapped children and adults from age three to twenty-one are entitled to these benefits. This does not mean that students who qualify for services under this law are going to be sent to special campuses, away from their friends. Yet quite the opposite is true. The way such laws are written, the students are to be educated in the "least restrictive environment." This means that the students have the right to be a part of the normal classroom experience as long as their needs can be met by means of modifications. Modifications are extra steps taken by teachers and staff to meet the student's special needs while being a part of regular mainstream classrooms. Disabled children attend special education classes only if a handicap is so severe that the child cannot receive an appropriate education in mainstream classes. If the handicap is severe, the child may attend special classes on the same campus or may attend a specially equipped school in the district with teachers and staff trained to deal with severe disabilities. However, these issues do not usually apply to students with Tourette syndrome. Most students with TS attend regular mainstream classes.

According to present laws, parents are entitled to be a part of the special needs educational process as well. In fact, students with TS and other special needs cannot be placed into a special education program without their parents' knowledge and approval. First, the parent has to give written permission

504 Plans and Aid for the Disabled

IEP

(Individualized Education Program): covered by an education law (IDEA); applies only to students who qualify for "special education services" in a core curriculum area; governed by strict procedures and timelines; parent involvement is mandated; schools receive additional federal funding for students receiving special ed services.

Both plans cover accommodations and modifications to the school environment and classroom materials, adaptive technology, and related services.

504 Plans: covered by a civil rights law (Rehabilitation Act); applies to all students with qualifying disabilities; follows an informal process; parent involvement not mandated; schools do not receive additional federal funding for services to qualifying students.

Taken from: Quest, MDA's Research and Health Magazine, 2009.

before the student can even be tested for special education services. Parents are actually a part of this educational team. They continue to be part of the process all the way through testing and appropriate placement. No decision is made without the parents' knowledge and input, and because parents have the right to express their views, they also have the responsibility of attending meetings designed to formulate plans of action to meet their child's specific needs.

For example, a student with TS should have a 504 plan or something comparable. The 504 plan is an agreement between the school and the student's parents or guardians for the purpose of helping the student achieve success in school. School administrators, teachers, and parents share responsibility for creating this plan. This particular type of plan is based on the student having some type of limitation that prevents him or her from functioning in normal physical ways, such as walking and breathing, and also in skills areas, such as learning, social skills, and behavior control. The 504 plan is especially useful for students with TS because the tics can occur suddenly, often in response to stressful situations, fear, or even sometimes for no apparent reason. This impacts the student's ability to perform successfully in school.

By working together, parents, school personnel, and the students are able to create and implement plans that help the student experience success in all of his or her school activities, both academic and social. In turn, these positive experiences help the student develop a healthy self-image.

IEPs

An Individualized Education Program (IEP) is just what its name implies: an educational program developed to meet the special needs of an individual student. The IEP is a very specific guideline for teaching a child with TS or other special needs. In fact, any student with special needs who has difficulties learning and functioning in school is a good candidate for an IEP and may qualify for services that allow him or her to be taught using methods specially developed for students with different types of learning disabilities.

The IEP includes measurable goals, both short- and long-term, for the student. For instance, if a student is struggling in math, a long-term goal might be passing the six-week term test. In order to accomplish this long-term goal, the student achieves short-term goals, such as passing weekly math skills tests. This could be further broken down into even shorter goals, such as correctly answering seven out of ten questions on homework assignments.

These goals can be paired with appropriate rewards. This is where teachers and parents can work together. Whereas stickers might be appreciated by younger children, they are not good motivators for students in middle school or high school. Thus, parents and teachers need to ensure that the rewards are age appropriate. For example, if the student gets seven or more answers correct on a homework assignment, extra time with appropriate computer games would be a good reward. This reward could be redeemed at the end of class during free time or at the student's home.

If the child has a need that involves social skills, goals might include time with friends, such as the student calling and inviting a classmate to go on a family outing. This is another goal in which the parents play an important role. They can help their child improve social skills at home in a family setting, and teachers, therapists, and counselors can provide support in the school setting.

Most of the goals and services spelled out in the IEP can be accommodated on a mainstream school campus. In many cases the services outlined in the IEP can be met in a regular classroom, which usually consists of a teacher and twenty or more students. Another option is a special classroom setting in which children with similar needs can go to get extra help. This type of setting is called a resource class and usually has fewer students. Additionally, the teacher may have the help of a classroom aide, a paraprofessional trained to assist teachers with the needs of students who have special challenges.

Although the IEP is the actual written document that defines the student's needs, the services to be provided, and how the services will be implemented, it is also the ongoing process of carrying out those services. The IEP does not begin and end with one set of services or modifications. It can change as the needs of the student change. For instance, according to an initial IEP, a student who has TS and learning disabilities may spend the majority of the school day in resource classes. Yet when it becomes apparent that the student has made signifi-

A student plays a computer game as a reward for completing work as outlined in his Individualized Education Program.

cant progress and, with some modifications, can have his or her educational needs met in a mainstream classroom, the IEP can be changed to reflect the student's changing needs.

The idea behind modifications is not for others to do the work for the student or for the student to get out of doing any work. The student is still responsible for learning assigned skills, but these modifications provide students with better opportunities for success. For instance, if a student's tics cause jerky motions, they can seriously slow the student's efforts to solve math problems. Because of this, one modification could be to assign the student fewer math problems at one time than the number assigned to the rest of the class. As long as the student is learning and understanding a particular math skill, skills mastery can be demonstrated with seven problems just as well as with twelve problems.

Tics can also interfere with a student's completing reading assignments. An appropriate modification for reading class might be to allow the student extended time to complete the assignment or even to have a peer tutor read the assignment to the student. If the school has teacher's aides, these people may be assigned periods of time during reading or math class to help the student read assignments and record the student's oral answers.

Social situations can be addressed in IEPs as well. For example, if a student is being teased or harassed about his tics in unstructured settings, such as the cafeteria, the school can provide additional adult supervision to address the problem. These are just a few of the wide range of modifications available to help students through IEPs.

Tools for Success

It would be difficult for most people to imagine taking notes or trying to read a paragraph while one's eyes are blinking uncontrollably or one's head is twitching or jerking. Because of this, some modifications for students with TS must sometimes go beyond extra time or the number of problems the student is expected to work.

Although modifying time for assignments and decreasing the number of questions or problems can help students with TS achieve greater success, other resources can also be helpful. For example, students who have trouble taking notes can use small tape recorders for daily class notes. In the evening, a parent or older sibling can write or type the notes directly from the recorder so the student will have a paper copy of the notes to study. In addition to taping class lectures, many textbook companies provide alternatives to books, such as DVDs, for students who have difficulty reading.

Tools for success do not have to be very complicated or high tech, either. Something as simple as taking half of an old file folder and cutting into it a slot that is the same height and width as one line of text from a textbook can help a student keep his or her eyes focused while reading. When the student finishes reading one line, he just slides the slot down to the next one. This simple tool can help a student with mild or moderate reading challenges due to jerky head motions to read more successfully.

A private, quiet space can make the difference between success or failure for students with TS. A permanent pass that allows the student to leave any class and go to an empty office, workroom, or classroom accommodates two issues: having a private place to let out tics as well as a quiet, distraction-free place to work problems or take tests.

Students with Tourette's may need special provisions like an empty room to provide privacy and quiet for exams and other assignments.

Additionally, for the student's own welfare and to protect the rights of other students in the vicinity, teachers can provide "buffer zones." Buffer zones are simply wider spaces between desks. This is especially helpful if a student has "touching" tics or whose arms and legs tend to flail during a tic episode, which could unintentionally injure students seated nearby. Students who are especially self-conscious about tics can be provided with study nook–type desks or privacy screens that allow the student to see the teacher but block classmates' views of the student.

Sometimes students are able to help themselves with their own creative problem-solving skills. For instance, when they feel tics coming on, some students can "focus" twitches by squeezing small balls of the plastic, puttylike substance that teachers use to temporarily attach posters to walls.

Tools for success do not have to be complicated or expensive. They can be as simple as a slotted file folder or a tiny voice-activated recorder. A successful tool is any object or technique that allows a student to function normally and comfortably throughout the school day.

CHAPTER FIVE

Latest Treatments and New Ideas Ahead

Research and development is a vital factor in creating more effective treatments and therapies for Tourette syndrome (TS). Treatments and medications that are in developmental stages today may result in a higher quality of life for people with TS in future years. Some of these efforts involve completely new concepts, but others combine new techniques with existing treatments, resulting in brighter futures for TS patients.

Clinical Trials and How They Work

The goal for drugs and other types of treatments is to relieve the symptoms of TS, not cause additional problems. For this reason, a great deal of background work takes place before new drugs and other types of treatments are released for public use by physicians and therapists. First, drugs are frequently tried on animals in a controlled laboratory setting before any humans become involved in the testing procedure, called a clinical trial. The type of clinical trial for testing these drugs, devices, or procedures is called a treatment trial. The purpose of these trials is to investigate a drug or other treatment method under carefully controlled conditions using human volunteers in order to determine the effectiveness and safety of the drug or other treatment.

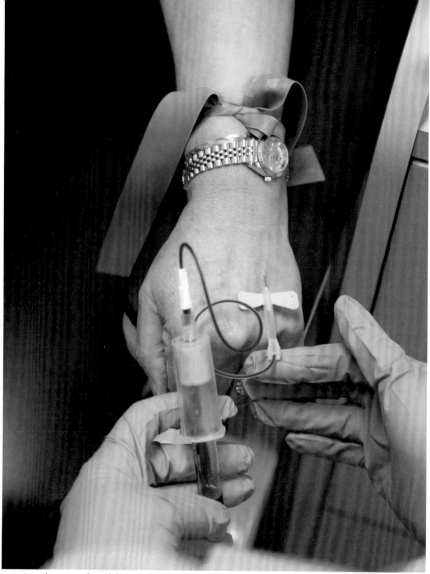

A volunteer has blood drawn as part of the process to participate in a treatment trial. Such trials are carried out to test new drugs or treatments for a disease.

Clinical trials work something like the scientific method that students learn in science class. First, something is identified; in this case, it is a medication or treatment device developed for people who have TS. Based on previous laboratory testing, called preclinical studies, the doctors and scientists predict that the drug or other treatment will prove beneficial to people with TS. Then the testing on human subjects begins. This part of the trial is like the observing and experimenting stage of the scientific method. The volunteers, called test subjects, have to meet certain guidelines, such as age and overall health, in order to participate in the clinical trials. For example, in order to be involved in one clinical trial involving TS, test subjects had to be boys or girls from eleven to sixteen years of age who had been previously diagnosed with TS and had a history of disruptive behavior.

Many families are willing to allow their children to participate in these studies. The treatments are provided to the children free of charge, and parents know that there is a chance the treatments being tested will benefit their children. However, in order for children to participate in any such clinical trial, parents have to give written permission and agree to provide their children with transportation to and from the testing center. Some of the volunteers in the clinical study receive the actual drug or other treatment being tested, but others get a different form of treatment or a placebo, which is a harmless, false medication sometimes called a "sugar pill." In some trials, volunteers are not told who is getting the actual drug and who is receiving the placebo.

This part of the trial is usually divided into phases. Those involving drugs are usually divided into four phases. For the first phase, the test group is usually small, about twenty to fifty volunteers, mostly from the same general area. This phase is to further assess the safety of the drug or treatment and is usually conducted in an in-patient clinic, where volunteers can be monitored around the clock. The purpose of the second phase is to assess how successfully the drug or other treatment works. This phase involves a much larger number of people, possibly up to three hundred. If a drug is being tested, this phase determines the most effective drug dosage. The third phase involves the largest test group, sometimes up to three thousand volunteers. Not only does this phase involve the most volunteers, it also covers a longer period of time than the first and second phases. Because this phase involves the largest number of volunteers, such issues as fine tuning the dosage and possible side effects are addressed at this time. If the drug is successful in the first three phases of human experimentation, it is usually approved for use in the general population. This means doctors can prescribe the drug for their TS patients. The final phase is called a postapproval study, which continues after the drug has gone on the market.

The entire time period of a clinical trial can go on for years. In fact, as many as eight years may be invested in a drug from the time it first enters the clinical trial procedure until it is approved for public use. Because of all the time and people involved in the study, including paid technicians who administer drugs and assist doctors in monitoring the progress of the volunteers, clinical trials are quite costly. As a result, many of the drugs and treatments resulting from these studies are very expensive, especially during their first years in public use. This is because the drug companies have to recover the expense they have invested in the research and development of new drugs and other treatments. Once the regulatory agencies approve generic forms of the drugs, though, the costs generally come down.

Special TS Research at Johns Hopkins

Clinical trials are performed and monitored through such facilitites as the Johns Hopkins Medical Center. Home to a 2009 Nobel Prize winner in medicine, Johns Hopkins Medical Center is located in Baltimore, Maryland. Johns Hopkins University and Medical Center has been the top research facility in the United States since the late 1970s. In addition to other research programs, researchers at Johns Hopkins have been involved in a number of Tourette syndrome studies.

One member of the staff dedicated to TS research is Harvey S. Singer. Singer is professor of neurology and pediatrics and the director of pediatric neurology at Johns Hopkins Hospital. The author of hundreds of publications and book chapters about TS, Singer leads a team of researchers who conduct studies in an effort to better understand TS, which could ultimately lead to finding a cure for this disorder. These studies involve different types of research into the potential causes of TS and how it may be passed down from one generation to the next.

One of these research efforts is the Buccal Swab Study. A buccal swab is a cotton-tipped applicator that resembles a cot-

Johns Hopkins: A Brief Overview

The original Johns Hopkins Hospital first opened in 1889. It was followed four years later by Johns Hopkins University School of Medicine. Since its beginning, Johns Hopkins has been associated with many "firsts." This includes being the first major medical school to admit women, in 1893. In 1894 it became the first medical school in the United States to use rubber gloves during surgery, a practice previously unheard of. Additionally, Johns Hopkins developed renal dialysis and cardiopulmonary resuscitation, or CPR.

Johns Hopkins has been the scene of many medical advancements and discoveries in recent decades. In addition to the Buccal Swab Study, for the purpose of gathering DNA information from TS patients, during the early 2000s Johns Hopkins made many significant contributions. One of these medical discoveries used stem cell grafts to restore movement in the paralyzed limbs of animals, which could lead to a breakthrough in overcoming paralysis in humans. Researchers at Johns Hopkins have also discovered a method of genetically altering allergy-causing substances, which may lead to the development of faster and safer vaccines for allergy sufferers. Additionally, Johns Hopkins has been involved in studies indicating that certain antibiotics, such as penicillin, may ultimately result in more effective treatments for neurological disorders, such as amyotrophic lateral sclerosis, or Lou Gehrig's disease, stroke, epilepsy, and dementia.

ton swab. The buccal swab is used to collect cheek cell samples from inside the mouth. In this study, researchers gather DNA information from the cheek cells of TS patients in order to study the polymorphisms, or genetic variations, in TS patients and to determine whether the presence of certain patterns of neurotransmitter polymorphisms can predict the tic-suppressing effect of certain neuroleptic drugs.

The Johns Hopkins Medical Center in Baltimore, Maryland, is a top research center involved in studies of Tourette syndrome.

Ongoing genetic studies at Johns Hopkins include research projects in conjunction with the Tourette Syndrome Association International Consortium for Genetics to better understand the genetic basis of TS. These studies involve families in which two siblings or a parent and a child have Tourette syndrome. Family members known to have TS are interviewed using special questionnaires to assess their tics as well as any obsessive-compulsive disorder (OCD) and attention/hyperactivity disorder (ADHD) symptoms. These studies hope to identify a region in the genome—all of the inheritable traits of an organism—which might contain a susceptibility gene for TS. This study additionally analyzes the comorbid conditions, OCD and ADHD, in conjunction with TS.

Johns Hopkins additionally has been involved in positron-emission tomography (PET) studies. Using a PET device, doctors and researchers are able to observe the functions of the body's organs and tissues to see if they are functioning abnormally. To do this, a tiny dose of a radiotracer—a radioactive substance—is injected into a vein in the arm of the patient. The tracer moves through the body and is absorbed by the organs and tissues that need to be studied. The patient then lies on a flat table, which is rolled inside the donut-shaped PET scanner. The scanner records the tracer with the help of a computer. This information is then converted into three-dimensional pictures of the body's organs and tissues.

For this particular study, twenty-nine adult patients with Tourette syndrome were examined by means of the PET scan. Part of this group had one scan, but the other was subjected to a procedure using two PET scans. For the first scan, the patients were examined under the same conditions as the other part of the group. For the second scan, they were given the drug haloperidol, which is used by some patients to control physical and vocal tics. The haloperidol travels to dopamine receptors in the brain. The test concluded that not all patients with TS have abnormal dopamine receptors in the brain, but some do. These results determined a need for further study of dopamine receptor elevation. In fact, other PET studies are being planned or currently are under way to investigate the uptake of serotonin or dopamine to determine if there are differences in people with TS and people who do not have TS.

As the top university and medical research center in the country, Johns Hopkins reported spending $1.7 billion on its combined research and development programs in 2008 alone. To help with the expense of research, Johns Hopkins has the Friends of Tourette Syndrome Research, a fund-raising organization headquartered at Johns Hopkins. Through this organization, people can make tax-deductible contributions to support the various TS research projects currently under way or in the research stages.

Some Controversial Treatments

Although many programs and studies devoted to finding a cure for TS, or at least minimizing its symptoms, involve conventional drugs and other types of treatments, others are more radical. In fact, they may at first appear to be counterproductive or even dangerous. Two of these drugs being studied are the botulinium toxin and a substance found in marijuana.

According to some researchers, the botulinum toxin, more widely known as Botox, may potentially be successful in decreasing tics. Most central nervous system medications affect the entire central nervous system. Botox is different, though. It acts locally, much like getting a local anesthetic to have a root canal done by a dentist. In one study, 450 patients were treated with a type of the botulism toxin. It was found to be effective in lessening the effects of tics and proved to be a safe treatment for the patients involved in the study.

Joseph Jankovic, a professor of neurology and the director of the Parkinson's Disease Center and Movement Disorders Clinic at the Baylor College of Medicine in Houston, Texas, comments on the testing to date of the botulinium toxin for the treatment of TS:

> While we have an enormous amount of data showing that Botox is an extremely safe and effective treatment for a variety of therapeutic and cosmetic uses, the important thing for patients is whether this translates into meaningful improvements in their daily lives. Our review makes clear that treatment with Botox accomplishes this across a wide range of chronic and debilitating disorders and conditions. . . . We have made tremendous progress with treatments, and even though we don't know the cause of the disease [TS] we are able to significantly improve the quality of life for patients with Tourette Syndrome by a variety of medications.[15]

Possibly even more controversial than treating TS tics with Botox, a substance used to rid the face of wrinkles, is the idea of using a substance found in marijuana to treat Tourette syndrome. One area of controversy is the fact that using marijuana as a treatment may have legal consequences, not only in many states in the United States but also in many other countries.

Delta-9-tetrahydrocannabinol (delta-9-THC) is a compound found in marijuana, or it can be manufactured synthetically. One of the earliest reports of using THC to control TS tics came from three medical doctors in Hannover, Germany, in the late 1990s who conducted an uncontrolled open clinical trial.

According to their report:

> Mr. A was treated once with 10mg of Delta-9-THC. (He was unmedicated and had stopped smoking marijuana three days before.) Using the section on tic symptoms of the Tourette's Syndrome Global Scale, we found that Mr. A's total tic severity was 41 before treatment and was reduced to 7 just two hours after treatment. Both motor and vocal tics improved and coprolalia disappeared. The improvement began 30 minutes after treatment and lasted for about 7 hours; no adverse effects occurred. To measure cognitive functions, we performed neuropsychological tests, which showed improved signal detection and sustained attention and reaction time after treatment. Mr. A himself noted an improvement of motor and vocal tics of about 70%. Furthermore, he felt an amelioration in attention, impulse control, obsessive-compulsive behavior, and premonitory feeling.[16]

A man with Tourette syndrome prepares medical marijuana to help with his symptoms. Marijuana is a controversial treatment because it is illegal in the United States.

In a more recent study, twenty-four patient volunteers, all adults, participated in a double-blind, placebo-controlled trial for a period of six weeks. Each patient was treated with up to ten milligrams of THC. The treatments resulted in a significant lessening of tic severity. In this trial, as in the earlier one, patients suffered no ill effects. This study served to confirm earlier studies indicating that THC is effective in the treatment of tics as well as comorbid conditions, such as behavioral problems without significant detrimental effects, like memory problems or effects on pulse and blood pressure.

Nicotine is yet another controversial substance under investigation as a treatment for TS tics. It has been known for decades that nicotine, which comes from the tobacco plant, has an effect on the brain. The substance is said to act by stimulating the brain's neurotransmitters. This stimulation results in feelings of euphoria, however, it does have a down side. The nicotine in cigarettes, cigars, pipes, and chewing tobacco also enhances cravings. The person ingesting the nicotine tends to want more of the substance. For this reason, smoking or chewing tobacco is not a good way to treat the symptoms of TS. There is a safer way to get nicotine into the body.

In an eight-week study at the University of South Florida, seventy young TS patients, children and teens, were treated with patches. Some of the patches were placebos, but others were nicotine patches, called a nicotine transdermal system. These patches looked like small bandages applied to the skin. For those receiving the actual nicotine, these patients were able to cut their dosages of Haldol, a strong tranquilizer, by about half. In some cases, Haldol can cause side effects such as blurred vision, drowsiness, dizziness, and even a movement disorder called tardive dyskinesia, so being able to cut the dosage of this tranquilizer can be beneficial. Another method they tried was chewing gum that contained nicotine. For many of the patients, their tics stopped within half an hour of starting to chew the gum. Patients reported that they were able to concentrate better. The children's parents reported that the younger members of the trial were able to handle homework assignments better and to read more easily. However, the gum

Food for Thought

A special diet will not cure TS. However, many TS patients have experienced milder and less frequent bouts of tics after modifying their diets, eliminating foods that seem to increase tic activity while adding foods said to decrease tic activity.

In recent years more people have resorted to special diets in place of or in addition to prescription drugs as a way to treat TS. Many nutritional experts recommend eliminating several substances from the diet, such as sugar; caffeine, as in colas, tea, coffee, and chocolate; refined and processed foods; and foods containing yeast, such as breads. Additionally, some patients try an elimination diet, which means eliminating certain foods for a period of time and then reintroducing them into the diet to see if there is any change in tic activity. Elimination diets frequently focus on dairy products, such as milk, cheese, ice cream, and yogurt, and corn products, such as whole corn, cornmeal, popcorn, and cornstarch. This type of diet works on the premise that if tic activity accelerates when certain foods are reintroduced, then those foods are probably related to the tic.

However, diet is not only about foods a person cannot have but also about foods that can be eaten. For instance, foods high in magnesium, such as black beans, raw broccoli, spinach, oysters, and okra, are said to be beneficial for people with TS. Organic foods are also recommended. Organic fruits and vegetables are grown without the use of synthetic pesticides, additives, chemical ripening, or irradiation. Examples of organic animal protein would include meat, poultry, or fish raised without antibiotics or growth hormones.

Corn products such as popcorn and cornmeal are thought to make some symptoms of Tourette's, like tics, more pronounced.

tasted bitter, and some of the children would not just bite into it and hold it between gum and teeth, as it is supposed to be used. Instead, they chewed it quickly and swallowed it, resulting in some stomachaches!

At this time, researchers believe that more research is needed before nicotine patches and gum are routinely used to treat TS. There is even talk of some synthetic drugs, similar to nicotine, that are being designed by some drug companies to have the same effect on the brain as nicotine. According to Paul R. Sanberg of the University of South Florida, "Now that we understand more about how nicotine works in the brain, we're looking for nicotine substitutes that could more precisely target specific brain disorders and have fewer side-effects than the patches."[17]

The Possibilities Continue

Today researchers continue to develop other new approaches for treating Tourette syndrome. Whereas some are about what can be done for the patient, others involve what the patients can do for themselves. Some are completely new therapies and drugs, but others are drugs and treatments developed for other conditions that researchers are discovering also benefit TS patients by lessening the severity of tics or decreasing the number of tic episodes the patients experience. These repurposed treatments include existing diets, types of psychotherapies used to treat other conditions, tests doctors are already using in the process of excluding other conditions, and even brain surgery.

A pilot study is currently under way to study how modifications in the Atkins diet, a limited-carbohydrate weight-loss diet plan, can be used in the treatment of TS. The rationale behind this study is that diet modification may lessen the tics caused by TS without producing the side effects caused by many medications. The goal of this early study is to establish the safety, effectiveness, and tolerability of using this form of diet therapy in the treatment of TS. This study is expected to be completed in 2012. Test subjects for this study may be male or female, ages twelve to sixty-five, who are willing to comply with these dietary changes.

In a recent study conducted by the Yale Child Study Center of Yale University, adolescent TS patients participated in cognitive-behavioral therapy known as anger control training (ACT). ACT appears to benefit adolescents with TS who experience bouts of explosive, disruptive behavior. Whether the behaviors are actually a part of the TS or are stress related, these behaviors can lead to a serious level of functional impairment. The goal of ACT intervention is to reduce aggressive behaviors and improve social skills. Two girls and twenty-four boys, ages eleven to fifteen, with an existing diagnosis of TS or chronic tic disorder were involved in the study. At the end of the study, parents reported a decrease in disruptive behavior of more than 50 percent.

Aside from controlling tics, scientists are developing ways to see how TS actually "works" in the brain. One of these studies uses magnetic resonance spectroscopy and magnetic resonance imaging (MRI) to observe the basal ganglia, a part of the brain where tics are believed to originate. These devices are already used by physicians to rule out other causes of tics in the diagnosis of TS; however, researchers have also learned to use these devices to actually observe TS activity in the brain. By observing and comparing the basal ganglia of people who have TS with that of people who do not, researchers can see how brain activity differs in TS-affected brains. Such information can be valuable in future efforts to cure people of TS.

Surgery is an additional approach to treating TS that is showing some promise. It has already been successfully performed by a neurosurgical team affiliated with Case Western Reserve University and University Hospitals in Cleveland, Ohio. The surgery brought about immediate relief of symptoms for a patient who had suffered from TS since childhood. The surgical technique applied is called deep brain stimulation (DBS). To perform this surgery, surgeons mapped the regions of the patient's brain using MRI scans and three-dimensional computer images. By doing this, they located the safest and most direct route through the brain to reach the cells that control the patient's movements. Then they placed electrodes around those brain cells. The electrodes supply a continuous,

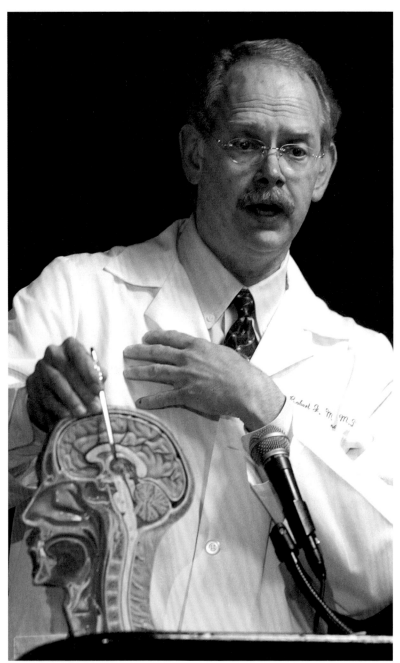

A doctor explains the technique for deep brain stimulation, which places electrodes into the brain to help control the symptoms of Tourette's.

high-frequency charge that controls the movement "messages" the brain sends to the body. These electrodes are connected to a small battery pack implanted beneath the collarbone by tiny wires that run just beneath the skin. These wires run along the scalp, neck, and upper chest.

Surgery is an invasive treatment, however, and is not necessary for most people who have TS. In fact, it is not yet certain how effective DBS procedures will be for TS patients on a long-term basis.

Other emerging treatments involve medications. At this time, haloperidol and pimozide are the only two drugs approved by the U.S. Food and Drug Administration (FDA) for the treatment of TS. Yet other drugs, such as tetrabenazine, a dopamine-depleting drug, have been used in treating TS-associated tics. In time other drugs, some currently used to treat other conditions as well as newly developed drugs, will be evaluated for safety and effectiveness in treating TS.

As more research studies are developed, more treatment options will become available for people with TS. Although there is no known cure for the disorder at this time, a research program in the planning stages today may lead to a complete cure for Tourette syndrome in the future.

Notes

Introduction: When Misbehavior Is Actually a Disorder

1. Quoted in *Sun Journal*, "There Is Help for Those with Tourette's." www.sunjournal.com/node/74125.

Chapter One: What Is Tourette Syndrome?

2. Quoted in Marlene Targ Brill, *Tourette Syndrome*. Brookfield, CT: Twenty-First Century, 2002, p. 27.
3. Brad Cohen with Lisa Wysocky, *Front of the Class: How Tourette Syndrome Made Me the Teacher I Never Had*. Acton, MA: VanderWyk and Burnham, 2005, p. 191.
4. Quoted in Elaine Landeau, *Tourette Syndrome*. Danbury, CT: Franklin Watts, 1998, p. 11.
5. Quoted in Teens with Tourette Syndrome, "Tourette Syndrome Today." www.teenswts.net/extras.html.

Chapter Two: Diagnosis and Treatment

6. Amy S. Wilensky, *Passing for Normal: A Memoir of Compulsion*. New York: Broadway, 1999, p. 2.
7. Quoted in Mitzi Waltz, *Tourette Syndrome: Finding Answers and Getting Help*. Sebastapol, CA: O'Reilly and Associates, 2001, p. 33.
8. Lowell Handler, *Twitch and Shout: A Touretter's Tale*. New York: Dutton, 1998, p. 49.

Chapter Three: Personal Challenges and Family

9. Quoted in Yale Daily News, "Study Shows Parent Training Can Lessen Effects of Tourette's." www.yaledailynews.com/articles/view/18215?badlink=I.

10. Quoted in Donald Meyer, ed., *Views from Our Shoes: Growing Up with a Brother or Sister with Special Needs.* Bethesda, MD: Woodbine House, 1997, pp. 47–48.

11. Quoted in the *Independent on Sunday*, "What It Feels Like . . . to Live with Tourette's Syndrome," HighBeam Research, December 11, 2005. www.highbeam.com/doc/1P2-1988306 .html.

12. Quoted in KATV, "Twitch and Shout Summer Camp, Winder, GA, Brings in Kids from Across the Country." www.katu .com/outdoors/featured/48214157.html.

Chapter Four: Tourette Syndrome at School

13. Quoted in Tracy Lynne Marsh, ed., *Children with Tourette Syndrome: A Parent's Guide*. Bethesda, MD: Woodbine House, 2009, p. 237.

14. Cohen, *Front of the Class*, p. 172.

Chapter Five: Latest Treatments and New Ideas Ahead

15. Quoted in News-Medical.net, "Botox May Be a Possible Treatment for Sufferers of Tourette's Syndrome," December 2004. www.news-medical.net/news/2004/12/21/6983.aspx.

16. Quoted in *American Journal of Psychiatry*, "Treatment of Tourette's Syndrome with Delta-9-Tetrahydrocannabinol." http://ajp.psychiatryonline.org/cgi/content/full/156/3/495.

17. Quoted in Tourette's Disorder: Information, Support, Hope, "Nicotine, Tobacco, and Tourette Syndrome." www.tourettes-disorder.com/therapy/nicotine.html.

Glossary

alternative therapies: Healing practices not recognized by the Food and Drug Administration (FDA) used in place of conventional medical therapies.

attention deficit/hyperactivity disorder (ADHD): A condition found more often in children than adults, characterized by hyperactivity, inattention, and impulsive behaviors.

basal ganglia: Structures deep within the brain that are involved in movement.

botulinium toxin: A neurotoxic protein created from a purified poison. First developed to treat a condition called lazy eye, it has more recently been used to reduce facial wrinkles and has had some success in the treatment of tics.

cognitive-behavioral therapy (CBT): A psychotherapeutic approach to influencing behaviors.

comorbid: One condition existing simultaneously with another condition.

complementary therapies: Healing practices not recognized by the FDA that are used in conjunction with conventional medical therapies.

computed tomography (CT): A three-dimensional computer image of a cross section of a body part created with the aid of X-rays.

coprolalia: Involuntarily uttering obscene or other socially inappropriate phrases.

copropraxia: Involuntary obscene or other inappropriate gestures.

desensitizing: To lessen sensitivity or reaction to a substance, condition, or situation.

dopamine: A neurotransmitter.

echolalia: Involuntarily "echoing" the words or phrases of others.

electroencephalogram (EEG): An instrument that measures electrical activity in the brain.

extracorporeal phantom tics: Touching or scratching objects or other people to relieve tics.

gene: A hereditary unit on a chromosome that determines traits.

homeopathy: Treating a disease or a condition using small doses of substances that given in large doses would produce symptoms of that condition or disease.

involuntary: Beyond a person's control, such as involuntary movement.

neuroleptics: A type of medicine that suppresses involuntary movement or other involuntary behaviors.

neurological disorder: A disorder of the nervous system.

neurons: Nerve cells.

neurotransmitter: A chemical in the body that carries nerve impulses across the gaps between nerve cells.

nicotine: The addictive substance found in tobacco.

nonobscene socially inappropriate behavior: The involuntary expression of insults, racial slurs, or other socially inappropriate remarks.

obsessive-compulsive disorder (OCD): A condition in which sufferers believe that performing ritualistic behaviors will prevent something bad from happening or cause something good to happen.

palilalia: Echoing one's own words or phrases.

psychotherapy: Talk therapy mediated by an appropriately trained health care professional.

serotonin: A neurotransmitter in the brain.

streptococcal: A bacteria that causes infections such as strep throat and scarlet fever.

tic: An involuntary vocalization or movement.

Tourette syndrome (TS): A neurological disorder lasting more than a year with onset before age eighteen. TS is characterized by both motor and vocal tics.

Organizations to Contact

Child Neurology Foundation
2000 W 98th St.
Bloomington, MN 55431
(800) 263 5430
www.childneurologyfoundation.org

This is a fund-raising organization composed of ordinary people as well as sports figures and celebrities whose children are coping with neurological disorders. Its Web site provides information about fundraising events as well as educational information about neurological disorders.

National Tourette Syndrome Association, Inc.
42–40 Bell Blvd., #205
Bayside, NY 11361-2820
(718) 224-2999
www.tsa-usa.org

This organization provides links to current information via its Web site and supports educational programs for medical professionals as well as those with TS.

Tourette Syndrome Camp Organization
6933 N. Kedzie Ave., #816
Chicago, IL 60645
(773) 465-7536
www.tourettecamp.com
This is an organization that supports summer camping programs in a traditional environment for young people with TS.

For More Information

Books

Marlene Targ Brill, *Tourette Syndrome*. Brookfield, CT: Twenty-First Century, 2002. This book explains what Tourette syndrome is and how it makes people behave. It also describes sufferers difficulty of functioning in school and how the disorder impacts families.

Brad Cohen with Lisa Wysocky, *Front of the Class: How Tourette Syndrome Made Me the Teacher I Never Had*. Acton, MA: VanderWyk and Burnham, 2005. Told in a first-person narrative, this is the life story of a person with Tourette syndrome.

Tracy Lynne Marsh, ed., *Children with Tourette Syndrome: A Parents' Guide*. Bethesda, MD: Woodbine House, 2007. Although written for parents, this volume provides information that would be useful to older children and discusses issues affecting daily life, educational needs, and the legal rights of students with TS.

Barbara Moe, *Tourette Syndrome and Tic Disorders*. New York: Rosen, 2000. This book describes many facets of living with TS, including associated disorders and laws designed to protect students with TS and other conditions.

Mitzi Waltz, *Tourette Syndrome: Finding Answers and Getting Help*. Sebastopol, CA: O'Reilly and Associates, 2001. This comprehensive volume includes such issues as signs and symptoms, related conditions, emotional support, medical care, and functioning at school.

Web Sites

National Center for Complementary and Alternative Medicine (www.nccam.nih.gov). The site provides information on alternative therapies and treatments.

National Institute of Neurological Disorders and Stroke (www.Ninds.nih.gov/health_and_medical/disorders/tourette .htm). This site answers many questions about what TS is, treatment options and prognosis, research, and related information.

Neuroscience for Kids Tourette Syndrome (http://faculty .washington.edu/chudler/ts.html). This site is specifically for young people. On this site, kids learn what Tourette syndrome is and how it got its name. There is also a section of important facts about TS and information about tics.

Tourette Syndrome Online (www.tourette-syndrome.com). Created by the parent of a Tourette's sufferer, this site provides accounts of personal experiences with Tourette's, pen pal information, chat groups, educational materials, and scholarship information.

Index

Picture Credits

Cover: Image copyright PHOTOCREO Michal Bednarek, 2010.
　Used under license from Shutterstock.com.
© Anonymous Donor /Alamy, 75
AP Images, 55, 68, 73, 85, 90
© Bon Appetit/Alamy, 20
Mark Burnett/Photo Researchers, Inc, 63
© Pauline Cutler/Bubbles Photolibrary/Alamy, 48
© Editorial Image, LLC/Alamy, 34
Mauro Fermariello/Photo Researchers, Inc, 31
© foodfolio/Alamy, 45
Gale, Cengage Learning, 29, 33, 70
© Peter Ginter/Science Faction/Corbis, 17
© Sarah Hadley/Alamy, 57
© medicalpicture/Alamy, 37
© MediVisuals/Photo Researchers, Inc, 13
© North Wind Picture Archives/Alamy, 14
© Nucleus Medical Art, Inc./Alamy, 9
© Thomas Peterson/Alamy, 87
© Randal Pfizenmaier/Alamy, 28
Tiffany Rose/WireImage/Getty Images, 52
© Chris Rout/Alamy, 51
© Ian Shaw/Alamy, 42
© Stock Connection Blue/Alamy, 82
© Stockfolio 538/Alamy, 23
© View Stock/Alamy, 44
© Jim West/Alamy, 78

About the Author

A retired middle school teacher, Sheila Wyborny lives in a small airport community northwest of Houston, Texas, with her engineer husband, Wendell, an assortment of rescued birds, and their Cessna 170 airplane.